Napoleon's Marine Artillery

JEAN LOUIS RIEU IN LATER LIFE

Napoleon's Marine Artillery

French Naval Gunners and the Campaign of 1813

ILLUSTRATED

The Recollections of Jean Louis Rieu, an Officer
of the Marine Artillery
accompanied by
A Short History of the Marine Artillery-1795-1815

Translated by Robert Bassett
Edited by John H. Lewis & Robert Bassett

LEONAUR

Napoleon's Marine Artillery
French Naval Gunners and the Campaign of 1813
The Recollections of Jean Louis Rieu, an Officer of the Marine Artillery
accompanied by
A Short History of the Marine Artillery, 1795-1815
Translated by Robert Bassett
Edited by John H. Lewis & Robert Bassett

ILLUSTRATED

FIRST EDITION

First published under the titles
Mémoires de Jean Louis Rieu
and
Extract of Historique de l'artillerie de la Marine

Leonaur is an imprint of Oakpast Ltd

ISBN: 978-1-78282-844-0 (hardcover)
ISBN: 978-1-78282-845-7 (softcover)

http://www.leonaur.com

Publisher's Notes

The views expressed in this book are not necessarily
those of the publisher.

Contents

Introduction by the Publishers

When we received the first communications from Robert Bassett concerning the material that ultimately became the book you are now holding, there was no doubt that we felt an immediate empathy with him for his endeavours.

His was, from our perspective, a very familiar story.

Robert, who has an interest in Napoleonic Wars, found that his curiosity was particularly peaked by an illustration of a soldier of a little known unit (some might say one of the least known) of Napoleon's Army—The Marine Artillery. This initial interest led him to attempt to discover all he could about that unit and, as is often the case, information was revealed to him incrementally, including in comparatively small, but intriguing, passages which had been translated from source material within the works of contemporary authors.

We understand, very well, the seductive effect of these tantalising morsels and the compulsion to hunt down those books that will yield all the elusive information the historical researcher seeks.

Of course, this exercise becomes the more difficult when the books that contain this information are not only antiquarian and rare, but are written in a language not one's own and in an archaic manner that has long fallen into disuse even for its native speakers. This kind of material invariably produces an English translation that is, if not all but unintelligible to the modern reader, then certainly one that requires the reader to put more effort into simply understanding it than many people would be inclined to commit.

Two authors, Jean Louis Rieu, (1788-1868), a Swiss officer of the Marine Artillery and Julien Felix Delauney (1848-1898), became the object of principal focus in this quest. Rieu, who revealed himself to be a personable man given to good humour and the occasional prank, wrote in his retirement an invaluable memoir which included detail of his time serving during the campaign of 1813. Delauney has left posterity with an excellent and detailed history which concerns the affairs and structure of the Marine Artillery. This material has, incidentally, been expanded in this book by notes which Robert Bassett had gathered together in the course of his own research.

As is apparent, by the very existence of this book, that all the obstacles notwithstanding, Robert set about the long and laborious business of creating an English text from the French originals. Having completed this translation to a point where he felt he had achieved all he could with it, he contacted this publisher to enquire if the fruits of his efforts might have the makings of a book.

This publisher has some experience in the creation of books generally and those concerning the Napoleonic period particularly. Indeed, we well understand the issues arising in the crafting of early 19th Century French texts into a readable English language form. So, simply put, a collaborative effort was quickly agreed upon, for we certainly believe that French accounts of the Napoleonic age are not so common in the English language that any which have been created should be allowed to remain in obscurity.

The Marine Artillery was an extraordinary unit, despite its lack of abiding fame. Its soldiers suffered dreadfully in battle in support of their emperor and his causes during the campaign of 1813 and by the time peace came after the Battle of Waterloo had, compared to the numbers that had served in its ranks, been practically annihilated.

As Jean Louis Rieu rightly commented regarding the last battle in which he took part:

We had, quite simply, been taken prisoner or killed at our posts and no one could ask for more of us.

This is an incredible story and one that deserves to be told so we trust that you will enjoy reading it.

The illustration on the cover of this book is based on the information provided by a watercolour uniform illustration by Herbert Knötel, of an officer of the 2nd Regiment of the Marine Artillery as he would have appeared during the Campaign of 1813. This and two other uniform illustrations were created especially for this book by me.

John H Lewis
Leonaur, 2019

Preface by the Original Editor

The memoirs you are about to read were found among the author's papers after his death and were the secret fruit of his retirement recreation.

Even though this story was never intended by the author to leave the small circle of the his own immediate family, it seemed to us, upon reading it, to deserve a greater circulation to a wider audience who might be interested in its subject, and so it was with pleasure that we, the family, eventually yielded to the many pressing requests which have come from those who would claim it for themselves and publication.

The great events of the First Empire of the French and the many changes of our national political life, which are described in these pages, all be it from the restricted but always attractive viewpoint of personal experience, cannot fail to interest many readers. Those who have known Jean Louis Rieu personally in his public life, but had no idea of his history will perhaps, upon reading his recollections, see him within the intimacy of his memories in a new and different light.

This is a straightforward tale, told in simple language, without any trace of vanity, but with the conviction to relate the truth in all the author saw and experienced from his own perspective. In these pages the reader will discover the real Jean Louis Rieu; the bad as well as the good, the austerity of his principles and his sense of playfulness. These pages truly reveal the strong character of a man who will not be forgotten by all who knew him and whose life and times are now immortalised for posterity.

Following the natural passage of the life of the author, the memoirs are divided into two well defined sections. In the first part the reader will discover Jean Louis Rieu's childhood memories and his military life, in the other the civil career. The first section was written in 1846, the second section in 1859. (N.B Given this Leonaur edition has been created specifically for the military history reader, this final section of Rieu's memoir concerning his later civil career has been omitted.)

We have faithfully reproduced the text of his manuscript and the only change to it that we have allowed ourselves is the suppression of a genealogical introduction, the interest of which is very special and in which some personal details appear which, we feel, the author would not have wished to advertise to the wider world.

Charles Rieu

Geneva, 15th August 1870

A Short Introduction by the Author

My intention in writing these lines is to relieve my mind of some of the memories of my family and of my own early life until the time of my marriage. Once I had determined to write down my memoirs I decided to begin the project because, I reasoned, if I postponed the recording of these memories until such a time when some of us begin to drool that would be too late. Memories, as everyone knows, eventually fade and then there would be a danger that they would probably be lost altogether. In any case, I might not be lucky enough to live to old age, so if death overcame me before I had committed these notes to paper they would be lost forever anyway. That loss, to be honest, would not be so great, because my life in itself has not been particularly remarkable. However, it may one day interest someone, especially within the circle of those with whom I am connected by blood ties.

I make no pretence of creating a literary work within these pages, but my objective was rather to make a simple chronological summary of my life and, rather dry and imperfect though they may be, of the phases of my childhood and my youth until the age when my spirit, which was to be fair a little precocious, was matured by experience. When that time eventually came, I began to regret having used so lightly and with so little profit those precious years of physical and moral vigour. Indeed, it was then that I saw that I had not amassed enough materials for my life as a man, and that I deplored this fault so common in many young people who neglect the present and entrust to an uncertain future the care of improving and perfecting their immortal souls.

CHAPTER ONE

My Early Life

When I was born in 1788, my entry into the world was, it seems, a great embarrassment for my Grandmother Turrettini, who was by that time rather old and who, to be honest, did not like children very much. My mother initially tried to feed me herself, but the absence of her own milk forced her to take on a wet nurse, and this complication to the normal order of things could not find an amenable place in my maternal grandmother's household.

My admirable Grandmother Rieu, on the other hand, came to the rescue and left her home in Rolle, Switzerland for my benefit, (Henri Rieu, the author's grandfather was the owner of a house in Rolle), and acquired a rented apartment at La Cite in Geneva. She then took me into her new home and devoted herself to my care until such time that I had been fully weaned. This act of devotion by my paternal grandmother was more commendable because (demanding in itself) it was made even more difficult since Geneva was, in common with several other cities and towns at that time, subject to civil discords. Furthermore my wet nurse, taken on in haste out of necessity, did not apparently inspire much confidence in her employers.

There occurred in the region, during the winter of 1788 to 1789, a taking up of arms, the main cause of which was disaffection among the native population, for the age of revolution was at hand, and typically this included the spilling of no small amount of blood. I, despite my infancy, was destined to be sea-

soned in these civil discords, for I have been told I attended them, quite literally in the arms of my nurse who was a woman of the people and so ardently sympathetic to their causes. She was, furthermore, married to a bad subject of a man given to similar inclinations. To the great despair of my grandmother, this couple would enthusiastically join with the mob when there was a riot and I have often been told my nurse might be seen in these affrays punching her husband with the fist of one arm whilst holding me aloft on the other.

This nurse of mine, Mounie by name, died in 1839. She was, by that time, a shopkeeper and had been living by all accounts quite comfortably. Upon her death she left behind some children including a daughter, (one might say, my 'sister in milk'), who, even today, I have the pleasure of seeing plying her mother's retail trade on a portable stall next to the shore gate of the lake. To be honest, the appearance of this contemporary of mine, who is now looking rather old and worn out, is a warning to me that time really does fly and that the amount that has been allotted to me is possibly very short and so I must take advantage of what remains to prepare myself for a better immortal life.

In 1794 the death of my Grandmother Turrettini and the outbreak of new political troubles forced my parents to go into exile in Rolle to stay with my Grandmother Rieu who had by this time returned there. My mother was about to give birth again, so I was sent on ahead of the rest of the family and this trip is the possibly first event of my life of which I have retained a distinct memory.

I was at that time almost 6 years old and was entrusted for the journey into the care of the usher Guignard; a *factotum* of my father. We travelled by the ordinary public carriage from Geneva to Rolle, which made the complete trip in a single day. I have still not forgotten the surprise I felt when, left on my own in the carriage during the stop at Coppet, I caught sight of the head of the venerable Guignard at a window of an inn eating bread and cheese. Of course, I was both inexperienced and very young and so I did not know what an inn was or understand that anyone could settle themselves elsewhere as readily as they would in their own homes.

At this age I was still rather delicate and I always found at Rolle the devoted care of my grandmother. But alongside the bloom of this gentleness the thorn of compulsory education was not long in growing. I do not say there was any problem with the reading lessons my admirable grandmother gave me, but it was a different story for those that came from the master of the so-called Latin school where I was placed to learn writing. There I was unfortunately compelled to study Latin, Greek and, I believe, all the sciences of the world, under the rule of a governor as ridiculous in his pedantry as he was by his ignorance.

The fact is I was too young and too precocious to learn anything. Nevertheless, I was by all reports 'taught well' though my father was, I fear, rather deluding himself in this regard solely based on the invested word of the school governor. All I had to show for this tuition when I left this temple of learning was horrible illegible handwriting and the fond memory of having pulled off the wig of my governor while he was falling asleep on his book. I also recall so complaisantly gazing at myself in a mirror during the geography lessons that I was obliged to cover with a cloth the subject of my distractions in order to remind me to give concentration to the four corners of the world.

Every year the two pastors from Rolle came in great ceremony to question the schoolchildren, and since they were both whist playing associates of my grandmother and my aunt, they regularly made me compliments which were addressed more like parents to a child. My little plebeian comrades noticed this distinction and gazed upon my aristocracy with envious eyes. Thereafter some of them seized every opportunity to get me into trouble, surely for the love of the compensation system which would ensue. One day, for example, the bag of books belonging to one of these little comrades was plunged into a tub of water next to where I was sitting. It was not me who put it there, I attest to the heavens, but the act seemed so pleasant to me at the time that I spontaneously laughed aloud most heartily.

The real culprit, need it be said, kept a prudent silence.

It was necessary, of course, that anyone who laughed should be punished while protesting his innocence. A formal complaint was subsequently addressed to my father, who made me appear before an assembly composed of the governor, the father of the plaintiff schoolboy and himself. Needless to say, that in the presence of such respectable authorities my protestations of innocence were not even allowed to be heard. I was held firmly convicted, and after administering to me certain fashionable correction, my too credulous and incredulous father made amends for the crime himself by paying for the damages accruing as a result of the allegations made against me. The injustice of the process was so deeply ingrained in my memory as a child, slight as it was, that I am still able to recount the affair in detail.

The only profit that I derived from this school was my friendship with a classmate who was very superior to me, Louis Manuel, who afterwards became a distinguished pastor at Frankfurt and Lausanne. I saw him again in Lausanne a few years before his death, and I rediscovered fond memories of him that a long separation had not extinguished.

My father also had the desire to teach me the German language and, after having made me study its rudiments with an old lady by the name of Aunant, a friend of my grandmother, he undertook the ungratefully rewarded task of teaching me himself because he spoke that language well. In the lessons he gave me, he acted according to the singular persuasion that when I stopped short in front of a word I could not translate, that I did so not out of ignorance, but out of some defiant ill will. This assumption, very erroneous, was honourable for my capabilities, but how many tears it brought me!

I can still see myself standing next to my father's chair, looking anxiously at the unfortunate book, the object of my torture, trying to grasp the word my father whispered to me for he was impatient and when I did not succeed, I received a vigorous bellow of exasperation from him. It must be understood that lessons thus given, work in the opposite direction of their intention and for a long time their reminiscence instinctively inspired in me a deep disgust for German, which I could never speak, but which I later learned to translate.

All these misguided and, more or less, odious lessons at least had the advantage of making me feel doubly pleased at being liberated from them. The attraction that took me away from study was the endless potential of roaming free upon the streets of our town, where upon I could not wait to distract myself in company with my little friends from the brook, though they, curiously, were just as envious of me on account of my imagined expertise in Latin, Greek and German.

Rolle was a city made for the amusement of the diminutive onlookers of my own kind, for the political regimes which succeeded each other, and then passed on, put in transit along its single long street a variety of troops attired in all varieties of colours. I can boast of having in turn admired Bernese soldiers, French soldiers and Vaudois soldiers, for I witnessed the first revolution of the country of Vaud against Berne and the invasion of the Swiss by French troops.

All this military activity regularly brought soldiers to be billeted at my grandmother's house. This was something of an opportunity for a boy, so I regularly insinuated myself in the good graces of the soldiers lodged therein, no matter the colour or construction of the cockade they wore, with the greatest spirit of impartiality on my part—which is a luxury confined to little boys unconcerned with grand politics. Indeed, I retained a soft spot for the latest comers, (*i.e.* the French) irrespective of the intentions of their masters.

CHAPTER TWO

My Further Education

In 1798 my father returned to Geneva, and having left the rest of the family in Rolle, he put me in a boarding house with an old lady we shall call 'D', who occupied the fourth floor of the little house, now named Grenus on the Grand-Rue.

Since it was his wish to place me in college, on his departure from Rolle my father was provided with a certificate of my literary and scientific capability which my school governor had given him. This certificate, written in Latin, was a veritable piece of pedantry and exaggeration and the inevitable revelation of this sad fact resulted in the pronouncement (by those qualified to soon determine the truth of the matter) that I would not be moved into the second class of the Geneva College.

Alas! My father, who took all this very seriously, had only one more cruel disappointment to add to his burden in respect of the education of his son. Professor Duvillard, after having addressed me a few questions in that archaic language, to which I replied in a deplorable manner, judged me at best fit for the fifth class rather than the second wherein, even so, I found myself in the lowest level.

A pronounced Vaudois accent and scarlet coat, the remains of a paternal uniform, (Etienne Rieu, father of the author, had been a captain in the Swiss Guards until the dismissal 9/9/1792), earned me at college a great deal of bitter envy in the beginning from my peers and while I did not worry too much about that I nevertheless regretted the loss of my childhood companions who no doubt yet played by my little brook at Rolle.

As for Madame 'D', she was a little old Moravian lady of religion, perfectly good and possessed of an equal and serene spirit. She had an only son, a young man of sixty years old, ugly and false, but always jovial and with a collection of old jokes that had all the appeal of novelty for me. He was the secretary of the civil registry and when on the *décadi*, (tenth day—ten-day week—in the French Republican Calendar), he had a bride and groom sign their marriage certificate on a kind of altar in St Pierre the malignant ones rarely failed to compare him to a little cupid.

I did not place myself in the front ranks of my class until the second year of my attendance, but as I always worked hard the prizes of good grades began for me in the fourth class.

In the second year I actually obtained the first prize for devoutness and I left the first class with the prize for Latin translation. But that my writing and spelling were especially dreadful hurt me deeply and I long lamented this gap in my first education. My father thought that by making me embrace Latin from my earliest childhood he infused in me, at the same time, the calligraphy and French grammar. In this he was once again entirely mistaken.

The prize for devoutness I spoke of, escaped me because of my dreadful solecisms; I was reproached for them and this somewhat took the shine off the triumph of a first prize. This prize itself was the result of an incident that made me superstitious. Having dreamed some time before that the subject of the prize would be the perfections of God, I prepared myself exclusively for this section, and filled, following the fashion of that time, my memory with all that had been collected from verses and passages on this subject and all that is said in the voluminous Vernet catechism. Judge my joy when my dreams were actually realised!

My character in college was much more shy than mild. I laughed and amused myself with intimate friends, but in the more numerous meetings I took little part in school games. As I knew how to avoid ridicule and preserve my dignity without being offensive, my reserve, which without that could have been a source of annoyance, only brought me trouble in the college courtyard when I first started; soon I was left alone.

I had several friends in my younger years who I entirely lost sight of or that I met later with indifference. The only childhood relationships, with whom I have preserved the '*tu*', are Prevost-Martin, Auguste Dassier, Martin (Charles) and the two Gaussen brothers. We should judge friends by quality not quantity.

Being in college, I usually went with my parents to spend the summer holidays at my uncle's home at Turrettin and the autumn ones at Rolle, at my Grandmother Rieu's house. (The Château Turrettin, near Satigny, ancient property of the Turrettini family, and at the time in question, Jean-Daniel Turrettini, the maternal uncle of the author.) These were my greatest joys. I have never seen the Château Turretin since without thinking of the immutable habits that prevailed there; walks, naps, readings etc, everything was done there at a certain time and within certain limits. My uncle, like my father, rose at daybreak, and, like him, distributed the sleep that was lacking over all the hours of the day. The readings he made as a family were thus changed into intermittent pleasure, as the book and the bells alternated with admirable uniformity.

In 1801, I was removed from Mrs D.,'s house and reunited with my family at No.118, (this was the 'Maison Rieu', Rue du Puits-St-Pierre),and in 1803 I left the college to enter the audience of '*Belles-Lettres*', (a literary circle) where I continued my studies until 1804.

I had there for teachers: M. Weber who taught Greek and French grammar, a man of intellect who loved nothing more than to talk and to tell, that, once that failing was well known, we regularly managed to side track him into talking about a certain journey he had made in France and England. This narrative could be scattered by so many episodes that they absorbed the lessons which otherwise would have been more demanding for his students. M. Duvillard taught Latin classics whilst M. Picot imbued us with a knowledge of history.

The studies then were done in a very relaxed manner, by

which I mean they were easily vulnerable to exploitation by us. So, nothing could be easier than to miss the lessons with impunity and more than once I went with my companion for a pleasurable walk while elsewhere the learned Professor Duvillard continued to wrestle with Tacitus.

What favoured such a leave of absence was a singular abuse in which, as the exams approached, the students obtained from each professor the authorisation to be examined *only* on part of his course. By a small effort I managed to eliminate from my preparations, on my own account, about half of the parts which were taught and I easily passed the rest of the examinations which earned me great approval which was little deserved.

It was in 1804 that my religious instruction was made. I was out of college at 15 years old and was then 16 years old. I followed the public course for Catechumens given by Pastor Bourrit, with my friend Alexandre Prevost. The unpleasant side of the matter was that, still filled with themes of religion from college, Prevost and I found it very tedious to have to hear a rather undeveloped commentary of the catechism, presented in a form that could be grasped by young artisans for whom this teaching was as new to them as it was old for us. The result was that we were less than attentive and spent the hour of the lesson watching and laughing at the nonsense that these young people answered when the pastor questioned them.

I must, however, exclude a young man called Guizot, a younger brother of the Minister of State, from this barely literate group. He lived in Geneva with his mother and the future Minister to follow the public studies, and this family occupied a tiny apartment in the old Dejoux House on Rue Verdaine, where I sometimes went to visit the younger Guizot. I have seen the elder brother there more than once, whose very modest entourage hardly allowed him to presume the high destinies which awaited him. (Francois Pierre Guillaume Guizot lived in Geneva with his mother who had come to the town after the execution of his father during the Reign of Terror. He eventually became the 17th Prime Minister of France.)

It was the old pastor, Martin-Gourgas, then librarian, who examined me for my admission to the communion. I remember that he asked me for the proofs of the existence of God. I tried to demonstrate that concept by the existence of the beauties of nature. The problem was that while doing so I was looking out of a window of a room overlooking the drab courtyard of the college, which was an uninspiring landscape well known to me. I would not have chosen, in ideal circumstances, that particular view as a preference to support my thesis. From a truly religious sentiment, from compunction, there was no question of the existence of God for me, but it was not usually on this side that the wind blew then. Few people thought about the matter or made others think of it, and I understand how difficult it is, when this order of ideas has not been implanted in childhood, to enter such a path later, and to openly make it a declaration.

UNIFORM AND FLAG OF THE STUDENTS OF
THE ÉCOLE POLYTECHNIQUE

CHAPTER THREE

The Polytechnic School

After a year spent in the audience of '*Belles Lettres*' my father removed me to devote myself to preparations for the (École Polytechnique) Polytechnic School in Paris. The school had been created in 1794 during the time of the revolution and National Convention.

Although I had not been consulted about this vocation, I could see the common sense of my father's decision. On my own part, my judgement was not still yet mature so I let myself to be guided towards a career, which did not seem in harmony with my usual inclinations, but by trivial considerations including the prospect of travel and the opportunity to wear a very elegant uniform.

Meanwhile, my brother who was four years younger than me, was already deciding for a religious vocation, which might not be considered very brilliant in the world, for other serious reasons and which proved his moral superiority. I had a lot of work to do to be able to take the admission examination at the Polytechnic School. It was necessary to learn plain geometry and algebra up to differential calculus exclusively, and as I had no pronounced taste for mathematics I had given its study little or no attention.

For my preparations I was put into the hands of M. Schaub, who was a Professor. Mathematics figured in public studies, but in an entirely incidental and incomplete way. Few young men applied themselves to it, and the professor seemed to have taken on the task of rendering the little he taught as arid and obscure as possible. The outcome was I could not benefit much from his teaching which would be considered very backward today. If his merit was clarity, then his fault was a tendency to follow the printed didactic book too slavishly and not to exercise enough in the application of the theories. This absence of less mechanical practice has never worked for me and, in consequence, this time was poorly spent for it left me weak for admission to the Polytechnic School in all that was concerned with calculating.

In 1805, after a year of preparation, I failed the terrible entrance examination. A renowned scientist, M. Biot, was the examiner and although he was very kind to me, I was, what we call nowadays, very 'depressed' by this turn of events. My competitor Gideon Audeoud-Suzs, who was happier than me to begin with, was admitted. The disappointment of my actual failure was not great since I had expected it.

In fact, I have to admit that had I entered the school I would have been too weak academically to have achieved what would have been expected of me and so would have been all the more unhappy. I was left to struggle for one more year on Legendre and Lacroix with M. Schaub and the following year, in 1806, I presented myself, no less tentative, but more absorbed with the rules and potentials of X and Y than previously, to two new examiners, both professors at the school, MM. Poisson and Hachette, the first a member of the Institute and a renowned scientist.

I passed my entrance examination this time, though still by a very mediocre performance. I was very good at geometry, but I partly failed on algebra. I suspect that under normal circumstances I would have been refused entrance if not, for political reasons, the French government had sought to make the countries newly united to France (as Switzerland was) part of the French institutions as much as possible.

Another Genevois, Paulet, was admitted at the same time as myself, and ahead of me by several ranks which was not so difficult given mine was pretty remote. I left for Paris, full of regret at leaving the paternal home, but still more excited to go and see what was happening beyond those mountains which had always limited my vision and I made the journey in the company of Paulet and under the aegis of his worthy father.

The Polytechnic School had been put in barracks for only a year when I arrived there. In 1804 the civilian school was transformed into a military academy under the inspirational motto, 'For the nation, science and glory'. That said the Emperor Napoleon did not like its pupils very much, who had the reputation, deserved enough, to be truculent and argumentative, and inclined to believe themselves to be a good deal more learned than they actually were. So he had put in place a military regime for the academy to master them, though, notwithstanding this guarantee of their better behaviour, he never visited the school himself, preferring to bestow his patronage on St Cyr, which was a nursery for infantry officers.

If this military regime was good for discipline, it was much less suited for study, and it must be admitted that the obligation to polish one's gun, to wax one's pouch, to sew buttons on gaiters and to do *to the right* and *to the left* did not connect well with the study of algebra and would not be of much use to those who were destined for the branches of civil engineering.

The students were thus formed, regardless, into companies whose non-commissioned officers were chosen from among the first pupils to be admitted, who were at the same time heads of study rooms. The officers were former soldiers from the Imperial Guard who were good people and good soldiers, but without any trace of education between them. This was, predictably, another disadvantage for dealing with young pedants who were disinclined to suffer the less than intellectual gladly. The *commandant* of the school was, it is true, a colonel of the Engineers, but he was more biased towards the military life than the scientific.

The day was divided as follows: at five in the morning a drum woke us up in our dormitories. We were distributed in rooms of eight to ten pupils and upon rising one had to make one's bed quickly and then return to the study halls at six o'clock precisely to work until seven-thirty. From half past seven to eight o'clock breakfast consisting of a simple piece of bread was taken in the courtyard of the barracks. From eight to two o'clock we were in class, or at study in theatres. At two o'clock we were presented with a dinner of little gastronomy which consisted of something upon an unchanging base of boiled or dried beans. From half past two to four o'clock our peaceful pursuits were put aside for musketry practice, except on Thursdays when one could go out to Paris at liberty.

Of course, this excursion was forfeit if one had to be on guard duty or if one was constrained by a punishment order. Those who did not take advantage of the outing, and in truth it was hardly worth the trouble, would relax in the school library, though it was rather poorly endowed with recreational books. Finally, from four to eight o'clock there was more study, at eight o'clock supper, then bed, at nine o'clock in the evening, with orders to turn off the lights and sleep.

Sunday began with a thorough military inspection, which had to be prepared for by a fastidious cleaning which occupied most of Saturday. Thereafter a period of leave from 10 o'clock until 6 o'clock in the evening. Some permissions not to return until 10 o'clock in the evening were, in turn, distributed to the pupils. Woe betide you if you exceeded, even by a quarter of an hour, the prescribed time for re-entry to the academy grounds. Then one could be sure of confinement to barracks and the swift justice of the academy police.

This life, as the reader might appreciate, was prodigiously busy yet despite a full curriculum some pupils, further behind in their studies or possessed of more zeal than the others, worked during the rare hours of recreation which were granted to us. These students were called the 'strivers', while others, more lazy, found a way to fruitlessly lose most of their time.

The military character of the academy was of course reflected in our dress which was a sombre uniform. We had a full dress and a service dress (*Grande Tenue* and *Petite Tenue*) worn dependent upon the occasion. *Petite Tenue* consisted of a blue frock coat

François Andrieux

Simeon Poisson

André Marie Ampère

Guyton de Morveau

with a row of yellow Imperial Eagle buttons with the name of the school inscribed upon them, black velvet facings, white cloth breeches, black knee-length gaiters, *gancé* hat. *Grande Tenue* consisted of a blue coat with white lapels, red piping and blue collar, black velvet facings white cloth breeches, knee length white gaiters, *gancé* hat.

As for the studies, we were separated into rooms of 16 pupils, each having his work space on one of the two large tables which furnished the room; a student sergeant and a student corporal had the responsibility of order and supervision. The hours of work were set for each object of study by a programme displayed in the room and the time of each class was also indicated. A drum roll indicated the moment when one went to the amphitheatre for a particular class; the teacher began by questioning a certain number of pupils on the preceding lesson; every student had to have his turn.

The quality of this interrogation was marked by a number of which the maximum score was 20. At the end of the year the average of the numbers thus noted gave the relative strength of the student and combined with the final exam to rank him in his place from one year to another or out of the school entirely.

Here are the teachers whose classes I took during my two years at the school:

For algebra, Labey, an object of ridicule for his awkwardness; I have never been able to understand that a man so dull and timid would have been appointed professor. He read more than he explained of the algebra of Lacroix.

For the higher calculations, Ampère, a true scientist with a European reputation, is very lucid but often very distracted.

For analytical mechanics, the famous Poisson, my entrance examiner, this one was the pearl of the crop in all respects, ease of speech, lucidity, knowledge, nothing was wanting.

For chemistry, Gay-Lussac, no less famous, stammering a little too much. We had in this branch two ceremonial lessons of the famous Fourcroy, I have never heard less said in pompous words.

For physics, Hassenfratz, former revolutionary and member

JEAN HENRI HASSENFRATZ

JEAN NICOLAS PIERRE HACHETTE

GASPARD MONGE

of the Municipality of Paris. He owed his elevation more to this distinction than to his knowledge; his calculations were learned by heart without him understanding them himself, he was a stutterer, which added to the fog of his science. He was so little thought of that instead of passing under a triumphal arch during his last lesson, we forced him to walk on one of his works, an elementary treatise of astronomy, the most pitiful imaginable, the torn pages of which we scattered in his path. We were reprimanded and punished, but the joke was no less biting.

For descriptive geometry, Hachette, also one of my entrance examiners, a slender little man, putting no interest in his lessons, not trying to be understood. Fortunately, he had an excellent draughtsman, a Mr. Girard, who came in the study rooms to explain the hieroglyphics of the professor.

We had two lessons from the famous Monge, founder of the school, on the aerial perspective; although it was only for observation, like those of Fourcroy, there was all the difference between the true scholar and the charlatan. His face and his gestures were of a nature to make an impression, and seemed to give a body to objects in space which, however existed only in his thought and by his word.

For the drawing of maps and fortifications, Du Hays, a good Alsatian, with an almost German accent, naive and heavy.

For the design of the bridges and roads, Sganzin, Inspector General of Roads and Bridges; he had no pretensions to eloquence and read to us, as quickly as possible a written course, then hastened back into his *cabriolet*, invariably dragging a great sword which, if it were not dangerous for the enemy, at least had the advantage of cheering us up at the expense of the civil engineer.

For Architecture there was Durand, honest and round, really interested in the students and apt to inspire the taste of architecture based on three guiding principles; simplicity, strength, economy. He had the talent to do on the blackboard, in four chalk strokes that he seemed to throw at random, traces producing an excellent effect. I am astonished that he left no other monument than a quarto book containing traces of Italian architects.

For the mineralogy, Guyton de Morveau, an old man, famous for his assistance to an expeditious procedure for the manufacture of gunpowder, which was so useful in the wars of the French Revolution. His course was not likely to add to his celebrity; it was little more than an arid nomenclature of small crystals, which he called out in a weak and barely perceptible voice, and it was supposed to teach an audience that was too far away to unravel even the colour. Add to this that, as this course gave rise to neither interrogation nor examination, it was regarded as an hour of relaxation where it was permitted to sleep.

For French literature, Andrieux. His course, which gave rise to only a few compositions, was, like Guyton's course, a recreation, but it was also fun. Andrieux was a small man with a thin voice, but sparkling with wit, his comedy, 'Les Etourdis' and his light poetry have made him, in time, a great reputation; we can say that he instructed us by interesting us and often even by making us happy. We cherished him first for himself and then in contrast with so many bored and boring professors.

Besides these courses were some practical lessons, for example a lesson in drawing the head, or after the hump, in pencil. This lesson, which took place once a week, was useless for three quarters of the pupils. In a room filled with models each chose what suited him, worked or did not work. No one was worried about the quality of our efforts and the professor scarcely deigned to look at your work from time to time and, when he did so, gave some insignificant advice.

We were also called upon, fifteen out of fifteen days, to practise chemical manipulation in the school laboratory. It was certainly an exercise that could be very useful, but the abuses and poorly understood supervision we received often paralysed the results, and if the materials supplied for manipulation were diverted from their destination, we were left to say the experiment had failed as if we had actually undertaken it.

From what I have just said one can see how much this famous institution left something to be desired both on the part of the professors and on the side of the pupils. Yet there was a *comman-dant* of the school, inspector of studies, military discipline and so on. But the first moment of zeal of this beautiful Republican institution had passed; the famous founders had disappeared and the genius of the war extinguished the torch of study.

The school then had, and I believe still has, a capital defect, that of over embracing objects of study, and thus to address national self-love by its universality rather than by real utility, in view of the public service, by its speciality. No doubt it was true, in pushing the higher calculations far enough it tended to develop intelligence to a certain extent, but it neglected practical applications too much, by leaving it to the schools of application; but we arrived there at twenty, that is to say, too late to break the realities of the engineering profession.

It is to this cause that it is necessary to attribute the superiority of reputation and fact which, in applications to the industry, the engineers who have left Central School have on the pupils who have left Polytechnic School, and the English civil engineers on French engineers.

During my stay at the Polytechnic School I was called upon only once to practice for a *planchette* survey in the field; the operation was going on between several pupils, the lazy ones copying all the work of the others.

I have already mentioned the *commandant* of the school, named Gay de Vernon, an officer known for a work on the military art, which is a compilation rather formless and without method, gathered in two volumes in quarto, including all the military branches for all arms, and for that reason very incomplete on each speciality. He had served on a campaign under General Houchard, who was his hero, and he drew inspiration from all his glory and his quotations. He was a melancholy and irritable man, opening his mouth only to grumble, which was his way to communicate with the students, who therefore hated him cordially. He was the cause of many small mutinies and of many punishments. I only knew of him by his sullen air and his presence in the professor's courses.

The Inspector of Studies was a M. Lebrun, a man already old and powdered to white, of an honest and gentle nature, that also attended the classes. Moreover, he made tours in the study rooms to see if everything was in order, not penetrating, however, into the very science of which he seemed not to interfere. I kept to myself so well that he had only one conversation with me in two years. I was one day cited before the school's board of directors; composed of the chiefs, military and civilian, for not having delivered to the library a book which I had borrowed. It was a minor peccadillo and my first fault. I arrived, bearing on my face the imprint of a much-exaggerated consternation. M. Lebrun reproached me amiably, kindly remarking that the crime did not warrant a death sentence.

Finally, I arrive at the culminating point; the Governor of the Polytechnic School, Général Comte Lamée de Cessac, who was circulating at the extreme limits of the school system. He did not live at the school, where he made one or two appearances a year. These were when we were engaged in exercises which were activities closer to his heart as a soldier. Then he could be heard shouting as far as he could with a very clear voice: 'Silence! Silence!'. One must not rush to conclude that we students were overly talkative, but only that the general wished to announce that he was there in flesh and blood. He was there, I like to believe, often in spirit, but in a world too far away to be visible to the naked eye.

Comte de Lamée had been an officer under the old regime, so how did he relate to the new? I do not know, but in any case, he had known how to put himself in the good graces of the Emperor by providing him with prodigious amounts of cannon fodder in his capacity as Director General of Conscription. We all know that His Majesty was very fond of this method of filling his ranks.

He had produced, in his early years, a little treatise on the service of the infantry officer in the field and this work is not without merit for its time. This governor, invisible in ordinary times, made himself visible on his birthday when some favoured pupils were invited to the countryside of Saint-Mandé to the celebration, though I never burned myself personally in the flame of this particular sun.

During my stay at the school, we failed to make any practical applications of what we were taught. However, we were made to visit, during the holidays, various public institutions and we were thus conducted to the Sevres Factory, the old Marly machine, the Chaillot fire pump, the Gobelins, the Catacombs, the Conservatory of Arts and Crafts, the reliefs of strongholds, the Invalides and others. In these holidays which marked the transition from one term to the other, we also made armed military marches and firing drills in the vicinity of Paris.

The pleasure we had in showing ourselves to be an object of admiration for passers-by was extreme. One day, a little tourist somewhere, during a halt, took one of our comrades aside and asked him if he was one of the young scholars of the illustrious Polytechnic School, the other replied with imperturbable *sang-froid* 'Yes sir, you are not mistaken.' We amused ourselves enough with this simple answer, in which, however, our self-esteem was naturally, if that were possible, further inflated.

In addition to this the Polytechnic School was twice called upon to take up arms while I was there. The first time was a ceremony ordered for the transfer of the remains of the illustrious fortification engineer, Vauban, in the church of Les Invalides. The principal the interest of this event, rather petty indeed, was in the speeches given at the Invalides extolling the virtues of the great man, but we heard nothing of them because we were ordered to remain outside, lining the street like a hedge.

The second occasion was the solemn *Te Deum* sung in the cathedral of Notre Dame on the occasion of the happy outcome of the Prussian campaign. We were, once again, made to form the border like a hedge though on this occasion along the Rue Saint-Honoré, and we thus had a close view of the parade of the Imperial carriages and their contents. The Emperor, wrapped in a big Imperial cloak, was at the back of an open carriage, which was harnessed with several white horses and preceded by runners attired in shining costumes. He had before him his brother Jerome, whilst another carriage contained the Empress Josephine and her ladies of honour, all duly made up. Napoleon looked rather bored in the midst of his glory and the military personnel present alone provided the majority of the enthusiasm for the affair, which the Parisian citizens hardly showed.

The courses of the school lasted two years; the transition from the first year to the second was by major examinations, which if one failed the first year of study, had to be repeated and thus one remained three years at the school. The second year also ended with major examinations. These were decisive, one was admitted to a public service, classified in the infantry or returned without a place if one failed.

As for the distribution to the services, it took place in the following way. The student, at his entry, indicated, in order of preference, the services to which he aspired. At the end of the time spent at the school the pupils were classified according to a merit number and each one obtained one of the services he had asked for as long as the places to be given were not taken by numbers higher than his. If these places were taken, it was arranged according to his rank in other services less sought after, even if they had not been preferred.

There were the various services, which I classify according to the consideration attached to them: Maritime Engineering or Vessel construction, Mines and Factories, Bridges and Roads, Military Engineering, Land Artillery and Marine Artillery.

The prevailing military spirit made many able-bodied students, by ambition and in the hope of a quicker advancement, prefer the military services of engineers or artillery to the civil services, which, by the way, offered to give far fewer places.

The courses of one group were distinct from those of the other, and one could live in the school in two different groups without knowing anyone from the other or exchanging four words throughout ones tenure. That's how I did not see three of my fellow countrymen who were at school at the same time as me, though none were actually in my year. They were Audeoud,

Dufour (later General of the Swiss Confederation), and Pichard, (a Vaud engineer); each had their own particular use of the rare hours of freedom granted to the pupils; the rest of the time, filled by study, excluded any liaison.

Besides, I had brought to the school a reserved character which did not leave me, and made me join only with a small number of comrades who shared with me the use of a room or study. It's easy to guess that I was not looking for garrulous or rowdy people. I worked a great deal, and needed to do it, because I did not have, as I said, a great aptitude for the mathematical calculations that were the cornerstone of the teaching. My natural shyness did not leave me with sufficient presence of mind to respond to the examiners, and I saw myself replaced by other students who were more lazy or ignorant but better able to face the questions.

This mistrust of myself has not been lacking at any time in my life, either when I was a soldier or in my civil functions. I can appropriately occupy a given position, but I do not seek to seize it. I am in analogy, in a word, wood, from which one can make a shield, but never a spear.

Circumstances, and not my will, have been able to put me in view by calling me to honourable jobs. Some people may have thought I was comfortable in them, but that was pure illusion. I have always left these positions with an instinctive satisfaction, to hide myself with joy in the crowd. It is very rare that the instinct brought in by birth is completely disguised and there is no precept or experience strong enough to smother it. I was, with this disposition, and in spite of my efforts, classified in the mediocre pupils and found myself very happy to be admitted, in a rather low rank, to pass at the end of the second year.

Now, during the second year, I was exactly what I had been during the first year which is to say hard working, but badly rewarded for my pains by the result of my efforts. A long time later, I thought I had a bad dream, recalling those moments of anguish in which, amidst books and notebooks, I was preparing to appear for my final exams before these formidable inquisitors who were to decide my future career. These illustrious scholars had, unfortunately, all the impassibility of the executioner who slaughters his victim; pity did not touch them. They were the famous Legendre, author of geometry; the Colonel of Engineers Malus, famous for his discoveries on the polarisation of light and finally the no less famous chemist, Vaquelin.

My success took place on the graphic part; the other parts were mediocre or defective. In a word, my examinations were rather more bad than good. It was not for lack of preparation on my part, I had prodigiously worked or *strived* as they say, but I lacked the presence of mind necessary to quickly grasp the question and promptitude to answer it, having eventually recovered the solution in the midst of materials piled in a memory which was too overloaded.

Alas! I had to resign myself to taking a service that I had not asked for, and for which the pupils, in general, showed repugnance. I mean the Marine Artillery.

JEAN LOUIS RIEU AS A YOUNG MAN IN
THE UNIFORM OF THE MARINE ARTILLERY

CHAPTER THREE

I Join the Marine Artillery

My parents would have liked the peaceful service of the bridges and roadways for me, whilst I would have preferred a career in the Military Engineers. My father, I am afraid, still cradled the illusions he had of my ability, which meant he always presumed too much of me.

By virtue of my age and by character I did not worry about much for long and the time that passed between the month of October 1808, the time of my return to Geneva at the end of school, until the month of February 1809 when I received my order of departure for my new destination, was enough time to reconcile me to my fate. In fact, I began to appreciate the appeals of freedom from guardianship and interminable examinations together with the small vanity of wearing an epaulette—both of which were consolations which offered themselves to my frivolous spirit.

An anecdote will prove the lack of depth of my dispositions and plans for the future. I packed my trunk for the departure of which I have just spoken, that is, to join the regiment of Marine Artillery at Brest. I banished all my books and notebooks from the Polytechnic School because they exhaled, for me, the intolerable smell of examinations. Then, along came my father, who, having always lived in books, considered them as necessary as the air we breathe, so, great was his indignation at the sight of these poor banished books. From there to over-ruling my own judgement on the matter there was no hesitation, and the order was given to me to include them in my scholar's baggage. I was not used to answering back to my father and I submitted as good sons invariably do.

I must add that my first movement was excellent, the trunk had already welcomed Lacroix, Poisson and some other learned companions, when my wicked spirit made me remember some hidden hideaway in the dark recess of a corridor in our home. O shame! I gave in to temptation, and emptying pell-mell the peat of my boring scholars, I threw them into this hiding place, condemning them indefinitely to prison, without even allowing them to call back to my father who, certainly, would have used his skill to recover them. I left them there without remorse, these unfortunates that I thought doomed to an eternal silence, but there was a providence in store for these innocents.

A year or two afterwards, repairs to the apartment bought to light the hiding place and its contents. My friend, Gaussen, has often told me, laughing to tears at the memory, of the profound astonishment of my dear father at this surprising discovery, but I was then a few hundred leagues away and quite liberated, so that for me the storm fortunately passed over quite unnoticed.

I left Switzerland for Brest, with very few worries in my heart in February, 1809, with the rank of second lieutenant of Marine Artillery. In Paris, I met a former school friend of mine going to the same destination so we rode together in the coach to Rennes, but we left it in this city with the admirable thought that it would be much more agreeable to take what was called the post horses. This more independent way of travelling had its zest for the imagination, but it also had another more real initial attraction for a certain place on my person (that shall remain unnamed) and which was, however, in a pitiful state by the time I arrived in Brest.

Here is what the service of the Marine Artillery was at this time when I arrived in Brest.

The corps provided the guard service in seaports, together with detachments in the isolated forts situated along the coast. Finally, it was supposed to provide detachments for the service

EMPIRE FRANÇAIS EN 1813

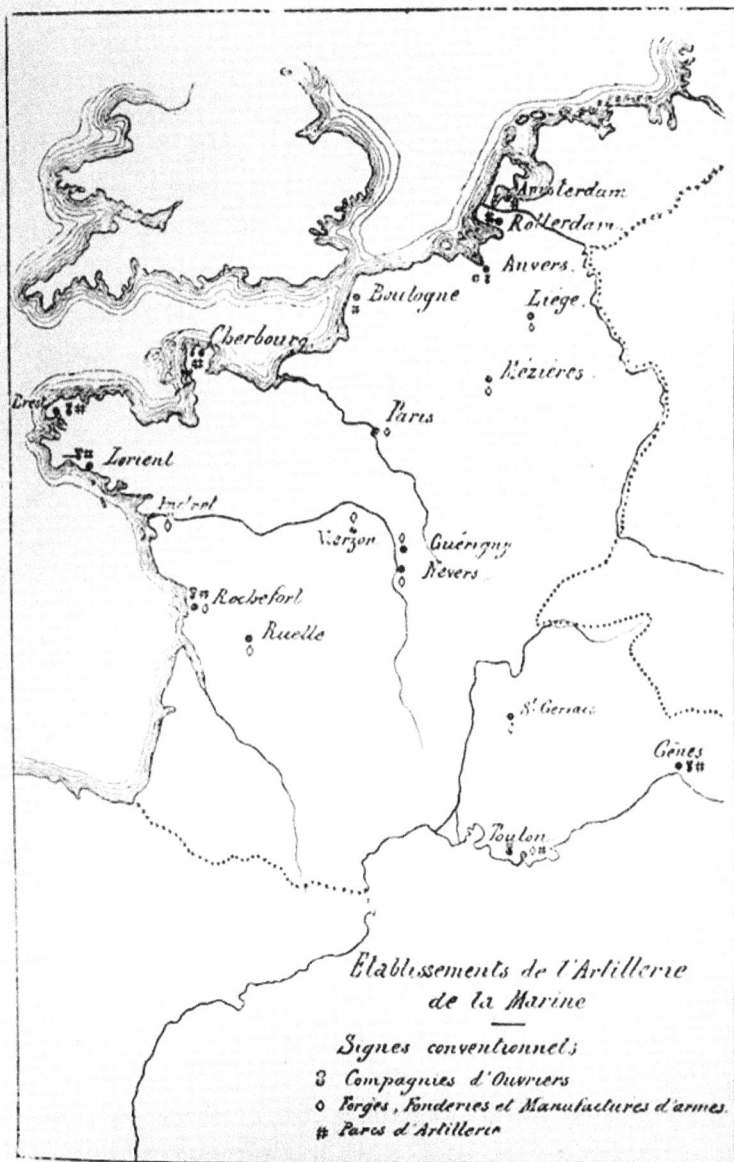

Établissements de l'Artillerie
de la Marine

Signes conventionnels

3 Compagnies d'Ouvriers
o Forges, Fonderies et Manufactures d'armes.
Parcs d'Artillerie

in the colonies and on the warships. I say 'supposed' because most of the colonies were in the hands of the English or having their communications intercepted by the blockade, so there was little question of sending troops there.

As for the warships, the services of the artillery had fallen largely into the hands of the naval officers and the sailors. Naval officers of vessels, starting with the captains never approved of any troops which did not report to them in all respects. This created an environment of reciprocal prejudice aboard ships and engendered conflicts between individuals and services. The Ministry of Marine in the end had to remove, on a great number of warships, everyone but a few Marine Artillery sub-officers serving as master gunners who were specially charged with the handling of munitions.

In 1810, however, this order of things, which was not well regulated, and revealed incompetence within the navy attracted the attention of the Emperor and the Ministry of the Navy. A commission was accordingly appointed to regulate the service of the Marine Artillery. The result was a decree which fixed the rank of the artillery officers and the strength of the detachments of this branch on board each type of warship.

The decree did not remedy the essential wrong, because it did not specify the nature of the service that these detachments would do once on board. It was, of course, quite natural for them to do the artillery service, but the naval officers, commanders and others, did not see it that way and that is what we saw on that day at the Scheldt squadron where no function was given to the artillery officers whose soldiers, like the sailors, were employed to handle the sails.

The continental war, by employing the navy's troops elsewhere, put an end to this badly understood state of affairs which could not have continued for a long time without some remedy. Today, naval artillery, greatly diminished in numbers, no longer supplies detachments to warships and a naval infantry performs garrison duty on these vessels. Artillery is only used in the service of harbours, arsenals and settlements. Marine crews manoeuvre the guns themselves.

This uncertainty about the use of the Naval Artillery regiments and the inaction of the navy by its inferiority to the English had, at the time I arrived at the regiment, removed all the nerve from this corps which was composed of old soldiers who were rusting in the idleness of guard houses.

The officers, almost all of whom had risen from the ranks of the soldiers were mostly married and old. The only practical experience they had been able to acquire was on the rare occasions when they had been embarked, but they had no theoretical instruction, let alone education. They were, in general, good people who had for us new arrivals the most amiable intentions. In this they were selfless, for between our rosy faces, our handsome manners, our new uniforms and their tanned complexions, their sailor-like looks, their rather worn out clothes, the comparison remained in our favour, at least to the eyes of the damsels of Brest. Of course, there was also our huge store of knowledge, the extent of which was not evaluated by the young ladies of the town, but by ourselves, and one may guess how far the fabulous self-esteem of ten or twelve former poly-technicians could go in that respect.

Naturally, the senior officers of the regiment should have immediately put to order the vanity of these young and presumptuous subordinates. They could have easily proved to them that they had more to learn than they really knew.

The colonel was what was formerly called a rogue, a man of intellect without morality, who cares little for the service and instruction of his subordinates and meddles with the administration only in order for personal benefit or to cause the puerile vanity of the officers to spend annoying expenses by innovating their dress.

What we newcomers straight from school needed, by example, was to learn our jobs as sea gunners, (a practice to us, completely unknown). The colonel instead contented himself by making us, *via* an adjutant; learn the handling of the musket, which we knew only too well, and so on.

CAMPAIGN UNIFORM OF THE MARINE ARTILLERY 1813/14

This uniform illustrates how they were mistaken for the Guard. Bicorn, blue greatcoat, red epaulettes, sabre briquet (only carried by *élite* companies and Guards by 1813) and the brass bands of the musket were all indicators of Guard regiments.

The dress of the soldier was, for him, a veritable gold mine, since he received from the state a fixed sum for each coat delivered. Realising the opportunities for profit he had found means, by a thousand little simplifications in the economy of the cloth, to actually get away with producing it for a much smaller sum to his own advantage.

I talked about the expense of the officer's uniform and this he did not simplify, because since an officer paid for his own clothes, there was nothing to gain for him. Therefore, he indulged himself in non-regulation imagination. Our uniform was initially very simple consisting of a blue coat with red collar and cuffs, yellow trim, blue cloth breeches, yellow cuffed boots and an ordinary sword girdle

Our colonel, however, added gold grenades to the collar, substituted the ordinary belt for a broad belt of white buffalo, topped with a gilded plate of fabulous size stapled on the waistcoat, with enormous guns in relief and, more marvellous still, substituted cuffed boots with heavy riding boots embellished with silver spurs. I must add that we had no horses when on the land and, were we ever to actually to be embarked aboard ship, these spurs had no function other than that of a bad joke.

The old officers, married and threadbare who had retired from the vanities of this world viewed these changes very poorly and grumbled to the utmost. We young men, by contrast, found them charming, for our serious reflections on this subject did not go beyond showing off all this elegant equipage in the *soirées* of the maritime *prefect* on the promenade of Brest.

A good Inspector General would have strongly rebuked the colonel and returned us to the approved dress regulations, but the Marine Artillery Inspector was an old man who had, I think, made all his campaigns in the offices of the Ministry in Paris, where he lived. He only made an appearance once a year at the regiment to count the men without worrying himself otherwise about our training. He would have had ill grace to give any consideration to our clothing, for he was himself very dirty and badly dressed.

ANOTHER VERSION OF THE CAMPAIGN UNIFORM

Here with cheaper black belts and with anchors on the sleeves, showing them to be naval. No epaulettes and a light blue plume, probably a company distinction for land service, are further differences to the previous plate.

Thus, went affairs within the French Navy and all that was connected with it. Napoleon did not like the navy because it was not successful in war and his omnipresent eye was therefore always upon the army.

Only the major, second in command of the regiment, surpassed the colonel. He was a superb man with an admirable commanding voice and unparalleled arrogance. I think that these qualities might have contributed to raising his rank, because the number of those people who 'stop at the label of the bag' ('judge a book by its cover') is always very large. But beneath the exterior was a vile debauchee, an unprincipled man. He had married a woman of good family and merit who he made unhappy by his excesses, because he perpetually sought to seduce other women and sometimes succeeded in the attempt. His audacity even went so far as to attempt his violence against a young lady of the good society of Brest; he failed on that occasion, but the scandal was great, and I do not know how he appeased the indignation of her justly outraged family.

When, in 1815, Napoleon returned from Elba, the major was the first to excite the regiment to revolt against the king. He was, therefore, upon the failure of that enterprise dismissed on the subsequent return of Louis XVIII, and I had heard that he ended by dying in a hospital for the insane; a worthy end of a badly led life in my view.

The deep disgust with which I was inspired by these leaders always kept me away from their sphere of influence and I was accordingly not generally in favour with them. A M. Musset, my father's correspondent in Paris, sent me some letters of recommendation for them, but I did not have the courage to make use of them.

The service to which the newcomers like myself were subjected was reduced to very little. This was the inevitable consequence of the lack of employment assigned to the troops of the Marine Artillery. There was a weekly guard to mount at quarters and a few rounds to do in the port to watch the troop in charge of the work done by convicts. Was that worth it to have learned

EXAMPLE OF A MARINE ARTILLERY CAMPAIGN UNIFORM

Worn under the greatcoat—a mixture of the old, longer habit and new 1812 shako

the integral calculus to come to that position? That's what I often wondered.

We were still made to attend daily exercise without giving us any command, which rendered the service uninteresting, and, what is worse, without profit because the habit of command is what gives the most confidence and consideration to the young officer. The other officers, with the exception of those of the regimental staff, such as the adjutants, mingled very little with the rest of the command; they were spectators rather than actors of the school of Marine Artillery. As for the Infantry School, which was a large part at that time of the naval artillery, they just took their place in the ranks when the colonel or the major reunited the regiment.

The time, which the young officers had left from their military duties, was rarely passed on studying books, as my good father would have done. In that one can build the wisest precepts, but when we see no possible application for our studies, it is a fact that we do not study. So, we shared our time between the drinking of coffee, attending the theatre and engaging in the weekly *soirées* given by maritime authorities, such as the maritime *prefect*, Admiral Caffarelli and Rear Admiral Bouvet, commander of the port, who divided these affairs between them. The good society of Brest was gathering at these events and there was often dancing wherein I even surprised myself to make a *reversi*.

The curious part for one who has never seen a port as magnificent as Brest, with its superb establishments and shipyards, is the sight of an armed warship. I felt that this life of a badly employed garrison had a lot of emptiness and I sighed for change. We will see in what follows that, if the change took place, it was often not for the better. I say it here once and for all by taking a look at my entire military life; except a few months later employed at instructive work or spent in the field before the enemy, I have found everywhere only the spectacle and the example of the vices engendered by immorality and anxious idleness, and if I had not removed from it a little experience of men and things, some authority in the exercise of command and the habit of

OFFICER OF THE MARINE ARTILLERY CIRCA 1813

Note the covered shako, greatcoat rolled over the shoulder for added
protection against sword cuts and fashionable Mameluke trousers

fighting against the torrent, if not to improve myself, at least to stay myself, I would have returned home *as meagre rubbish*.

Chapter Four

On the Northern Coast

It was, therefore, with pleasure that I followed, in the spring of 1809, my regiment which had been sent to guard the coastline near Brest because of anxiety arising from the discovery of a considerable gathering of forces in the ports of England. It transpired that this was the enemy expedition which seized Flushing in the Netherlands though it failed in its main object, which was to take Antwerp (The Walcheren Expedition).

I was quartered with the company I belonged to in a village called St. Matthieu, with the advantage of two coastal batteries and the ruins of an abbey abandoned to the revolution. It seemed to me that the boundless ocean that we saw before us would inevitably bring us English to fight and consequently exploits of prodigious bravery to perform on my part, which made my heart beat faster for youth doubts nothing.

This new life was a pleasant diversion to that of a garrison; we visited each other from cantonment to cantonment when we were not practising the more serious business of warfare on the coast. The thinkers among us studied the manners of the Breton peasants, a race of little men, true Celts, speaking an unintelligible language who were perpetually filthy and suffering from hereditary scabies. Nothing can be imagined less comfortable than their homes and therefore, by association, our living conditions when in their company.

On holidays we sometimes were persuaded to join in with their slow moving country dances and in traditional tunes whose musical colour was not exactly of the first merit. When we stepped onto the dance-floor we took care to put on gloves, not only to appear like dandies, but motivated by a prudence which one will appreciate, given the previously described considerations of hygiene, without difficulty.

My country pleasures were interrupted by an order I received, to my great satisfaction, to be part of a detachment of two companies sent to Boulogne-sur-Mer where the regiment already had a battalion. The reason for this was that Boulogne had been stripped of troops to send them to Antwerp when the English expedition had fallen back on Flushing and they were replaced in this manner.

The captain of the new company in which I was ranked added to his name a more or less legitimate one, and said he was the nephew of a famous general, a victim of the revolution. I express doubt here because a love of truth was not his forte, though he was otherwise an amiable man, but without any principle, having only a superficial education and more than doubtful integrity.

I was on very good terms with him and I do not hide the fact that his jokes sometimes amused me, but it was my responsibility that I not interfere with the service or the administration of the company because the dear man liked certain abuses in which he preferred that I was not a confidant. He also had the taste and the talent to insinuate himself with his superiors by the facility of his society and his cajoleries when they did not look too closely into his affairs and finally he was a great debt maker and a seducer of women. I have since learned that he died with the reputation as being a knight of industry.

I was in potentially bad company, but my cold and reserved character and the small dose of judgement I had received from nature, helped by my early education, always protected me from the contagion of these garrison vices. It soon became clear that these diversions had no hold on me and their corrupt proponents left me alone in desperation. This, however, proves how much the parents who aspire to a military career for their chil-

Napoleon at Boulogne

dren make them run moral dangers even more formidable than the chances of combat.

The detachment arrived at Boulogne at the end of August 1809 and we received an excellent reception from the new comrades whom we found there. The battalion of our arm occupied a small barracks camp backed by the port, but the two newly arrived companies were immediately sent along the coast a distance of half a league, one on the right, the other on the left of Boulogne, to serve as shore batteries to fire on English cruisers when and if they approached too closely.

My company also occupied a fort named Mont-de-Couple, and what portion of us that was not quartered there was distributed in barracks behind the shore batteries. Our main service was, therefore, to fire at long range on any English ship that could be reached. I say reached, because, the difficulty of estimating the distance at sea and the uncertainty of long range shooting made the chances of reaching our goal almost nil. So, to scare off a cruiser of the Royal Navy with a demonstration of aggressive intent was considered enough.

In this respect, our service was reduced to doing very little and it was the same with that of the battalion at Boulogne. The officers rarely changed out of *bourgeoise* dress and did not stay at the camp with the troops who were abandoned to the direction of a deputy non-commissioned officer and went off to do some rounds in the port. My captain spent his time hunting, and, detached as we were, we had a room in common in the city where we slept very frequently to go into society the more conveniently.

The *chef de battalion*, named Bertrand, was a man of the world, not very military and not very demanding; I would be wrong to criticize him for this fact, for he was always obliging and kind to me. I met him again serving in the Army of Germany, appointed *Général de Brigade*, and then he showered me with friendships and made me a thousand offers of services which I never had the opportunity from which to profit.

Before leaving the short chapter of our service, I will give the uninformed another small example of our military laxity. The post of officer of the guard was, during my stay in Boulogne, rarely occupied, because, as I said the service was reduced to rounds. The officers were, nevertheless, very angry with this inconvenience and understandably most disdaining the population of rats which occupied the guard house so rented, at common cost, in the neighbourhood a good *bourgeoise* room where they spent the night on guard, between two clean sheets upon an excellent bed. Despite this luxury and dereliction of duty they complained mightily about their inconveniences. By the employment of their social relations and because they were so well versed in chapter with the higher authorities the meagre service which was required of them did not endure and it was thus suppressed.

Here are some more examples of how we actually served.

When my company occupied the coastal batteries, an English frigate approached near enough that we were able to fire on her. At that moment there was not a captain or lieutenant at the post and an uneducated sergeant believed he was doing a fine and thorough job by putting thirty pounds of powder in a mortar which was meant to be loaded with just twelve pounds. The result of the subsequent ignition was that the mortar, which was made of bronze, was cracked along all of its length. My captain wrote a report on this incident, observing that the melting of the innocent mortar indicated that it was of faulty manufacture since it had not resisted a charge.

Needless to comment, he was careful not to say the quota of powder employed, but that he assumed it to be of the standard measure. The Colonel-Inspector of the Artillery took all of this to be accurate, and the mortar, which was new, was duly returned to the smelter accompanied by a very severe reprimand and the consequential loss to him of his perfectly serviceable mortar cast.

At the holiday of Saint-Barbe, which is celebrated together with the officers of the land artillery, one of our old captains was so drunk that, leaving the celebrations to return to the camp on

A FRENCH MILITARY CAMP

the right where his company was detached and not seeing his way clearly through the haze of his brain, he imagined nothing better than showing everyone the list of the passwords he had been given for the fortnight, taking it for the legitimate thread that was to pull him from the labyrinth where he was engaged rather than any serious breach of military security.

The year following my arrival at Boulogne in May 1810, we had a visit from the Emperor accompanied by the new Empress, Marie-Louise. I never saw Napoleon so close as upon this occasion, for, arriving in the carriage from Dunkirk, he found us ranged in battle order along the road, and since he did not have his saddle horse, he walked, in his grey coat, in front of our ranks. A few hours later he came to visit the fort occupied by my company and I had the honour of seeing him reprimand, with great severity for a small error, a poor colonel of the land artillery. This, as it transpired, was the same officer who had so happily observed the crack in our mortar. The tirade was basically a pretext to give vent to the bad mood he exhibited during his stay in Boulogne, during which time he did not accept an invitation to any of the parties prepared at great expense for his reception.

This visit gave rise to an incident, the consequence of which was the displacement of my company which joined the rest of the battalion at Boulogne. Here are the facts of the affair.

The camp on the left, and consequently the one where my company was, came under the orders of a *Général de Brigade*. This officer, an intelligent and a very intriguing man, had hoped that the passage of the Emperor in his vicinity would be for him an occasion for personal advancement. He was disappointed in his hopes, and conceived so much irritation that one morning he held his pistol to a fisherman's throat to persuade him to convey him to an English brig which was cruising before Boulogne.

My dear captain had, according to his custom, sought to ingratiate himself with this general, with whom he had become intimate, so, great was his disappointment when he saw the abrupt end of this liaison as it sailed away with the enemy. I even amused myself a little by chirping in his ear, telling him of the possibility of looking for the deserter's friends, a suggestion which he laughed at, but through somewhat gritted teeth.

In the same year, our *chef de battalion*, Bertrand, was called to serve in Spain and was replaced by another from the Army of Germany named M. Bléhé. The latter was certainly more military than the former and to our great alarm he began his reign by giving us lessons in theory, and by obliging us to go and sleep at the camp with the troops. This lasted for a few weeks, but our anti-military habits were too well ingrained and too seductive; the good man lost his latin, and was soon himself dragged by the current, so everything went back into the usual comfortable rut.

Overall, my stay at Boulogne appears in my short garrison life as the most agreeable portion. The officers of the Naval Artillery were privileged for admission to good society, which was not entered by the officers of the army and this good society was perfectly agreeable. In the winter there was a lot of dancing, in the summer there were many parties in the country houses. I always went to these events in *bourgeois* costume, and ended up forgetting in these pleasures that I was actually a soldier.

My fellow officers were composed of two-thirds of non-presentable cubs, but the rest were very sociable gentlemen, at the head of which were two first lieutenants, still young, though much older than myself. They were named de Coisy and Collot. The first is now at the head of the arm as a Lieutenant General, Inspector of Personnel and Equipment. In his younger days he was then a very nice-looking boy, much more involved in his own pleasures than military service, and having a marvellous talent for putting himself forward, and ingratiating himself to the superiors; it is surely this talent that has given him such a fine position. He used it one day in a moment of great embarrassment. General Vandamme, being abrupt, temperamental and unpopular had been sent by the Emperor, following his visit to Boulogne to take command of the troops.

One fine day an order of the said general appeared instructing the immediate removal of all moustaches and side whiskers. Here is de Coisy, sporting very charming side whiskers which he was constantly caressing and very disinclined to part company with them. Without hesitation he went to the general, to whom according to his custom, he had made a diligent court, and pleaded the cause of his side whiskers, for he did not wear a moustache. He won his case for himself and so for all others on the matter. I have reason to believe that the moustaches also had their reprieve, for the whims of the general on the subject of facial hair had, one may speculate, no particularly deep roots.

Collot was killed in 1813 at the Battle of Dresden. I do not speak of my comrades from the Polytechnic School, they all remained in Brest. I did not have, as we see, any more opportunity of learning my profession at Boulogne than at Brest, but I think it would have been the same everywhere. The Navy, in all its branches, was neglected and decaying. However, I sought as far as I could the rare opportunities of learning something and I read some instructive works, but the practice was wanting and for a young man the voluntary work is never of the worth of the work imposed. My dear father, who had been much more virtuous in this respect during his military career than I, always inquired with solicitude of my studies and found that the history of my pleasures took up too much space in my correspondence.

As everything in this world comes to an end, my enjoyments at Boulogne also concluded and in March, 1811, the company of which I was a part was ordered to embark on the Scheldt squadron and to return accordingly to Antwerp.

CHAPTER FIVE

The Low Countries

The squadron consisted of three ships of eighty guns, ten of seventy-four and three frigates; the crews were some French, others Danish and Dutch. My lot was to be embarked first on the flagship *Charlemagne*.

The vice-admiral was the Count de Missiessy, a sailor known for an expedition to the West Indies where he had taken on some of the English. He was an old man, with a courteous and polished demeanour. I remember that, having invited me to his table one day, he complained with tender sympathy that my learned studies at the Polytechnic School had found no other occupation than the Marine Artillery. He was correct, because the life I led on board ship was that of a cannoneer, having no service to do and no other concern other than drinking, eating and going on excursions in the villages bordering the road stead of Flushing where the squadron was anchored in a fixed position and blocked from the seaways by the English.

I remained only a month in this position, for at the end of this time I took the command of a hundred men put on board another vessel of the squadron, the *Duguesclin*, commanded by Captain Robin and there my tribulations began.

I have already commented how ill-defined and unpleasant the service of a Marine Artillery officer on board a ship was; wrestling with the naval officers who substituted their authority over one's own soldiers, and treating them like the crew's sailors, punishing them with pleasure and even striking them. Captain

Robin was not malevolent to me, but placed under the influence of his officers on board, and dominated by his own habits he did not give me the position and the authority to which I would have been entitled. This drove me more than once to acts of resistance and displays of bad temper that were not normally in my character. The sailors' career can probably become very interesting when sailing and navigating the sea, but in the harbour and the anchorage it is a trivial thing in my opinion.

The captain of a frigate and the first naval lieutenant alone had the proper rooms on board; the other officers were each housed in an artificial chamber formed by a canvas curtain between two guns; this room had just enough space for a small hammock and a chair.

At daybreak we were awakened by the cleaning of the vessel, executed with great noise and with a great deal of water thrown on the decks which were then scrubbed by the sailors. Then came, from time to time, battle drills where all the canvas chambers disappeared as well as the hammocks, effects and trunks, which were thrown to the bottom of the hold, and which were returned to you later in a state of great distress. Then, finally, the idea of this species of captivity, constantly in the presence of the same persons, often very disagreeable and the feeling of idle invalidity attached to my service in particular, all this, united to the seasickness from the peaceful ships movement predisposed me very badly to the life of a sailor, and made me sincerely regret the departure from my happy life at Boulogne.

I would be unjust, however, if I do not say that I had pleasant relationships with some naval officers, literate and well-educated, with whom I spent happy moments in the midst of other troubles, and that as acquired concepts are always a pleasure for the human mind, those which I took from the details of a ship, its manoeuvre and its discipline, although they were very imperfect, were an acquisition of which I could congratulate myself.

In July, 1811, about 5 months after my embarkation, a new order came to make me leave the Scheldt squadron, then composed of twenty-two battleships. I was appointed, along with seventeen other officers of my arm, to organise a battalion of recruits on the island of Walcheren to complete the regiment.

It is satisfying to say, when the Emperor had visited the coast he had been so pleased with the appearance of the corps of Marine Artillery, composed of old soldiers, which was becoming a rarity in his armies decimated by the war, that, far from ordering their dismissal as the naval officers demanded, he had instead ordered the completion and even an increase in their number.

Having disembarked on 20 July, 1811, I stayed on the island of Walcheren, living successively in Flushing—then very damaged by the English expedition in 1810, Middlebourg and Terveer. We were expecting conscripts who did not arrive and a fever which did not arrive either, although it had exterminated the English Army as indeed it usually desolated both natives and foreigners on this unhealthy island.

Finally, the following September 1st, the expected conscripts having received another destination, I was sent, with my comrades in service, to the island of Ré, where I arrived at the end of September 1811. There, as well as in the neighbouring island of Oléron, we were employed in recruiting and training in carrying arms, about eight hundred conscripts chosen from a depot composed of refractories from the south of France. That is, we did not have a choice of very well motivated men, all the more especially since, having to draw these soldiers from the infantry corps where they had already been incorporated for some time, their superiors sought by every possible means to allocate their worst subjects to us.

The inhabitants of Ré and Oléron have simple and primitive manners which, in general, made our relations with them pleasant and I have preserved a good memory of them. We left them on the 1st of April, 1812, with our refractory conscripts who had hardly touched the continent than they began to desert in large numbers. So many absconded that our poor battalion was reduced by nearly half or at least a good one third. Desertion was, in the south, favoured by the inhabitants and it was only at Poitiers, where a decree from the Emperor, pronouncing the

Napoleon and Marie Louise at Antwerp

death penalty against deserters of this category, was executed against a conscript, that the trouble stopped.

It took us thirty-seven days to reach the place of our destination, Antwerp, where we arrived on May 8th, 1812.

I forgot to say that on April 1st I had been raised by seniority to the rank of 1st Lieutenant.

The detachment that we were conducting was immediately distributed on the squadron's ships and the officers re-joined their corps or were also embarked. As for me, whose sailors' enthusiasm was entirely over, I was delighted to accept the offer made to me by the *chef de battalion* named Coupe, Director of the artillery of the port, to get me attached to his command. At the same time, I saw an opportunity to educate myself, and we know that these occasions had been rare for me. But here too my hopes were partly disappointed; M. Coupe was an original, not without instruction or knowledge in his branch, but not having all the leadership and judgement that would otherwise have made him a distinguished officer.

The Emperor, on his last trip to Antwerp, had an interview with him, and in general, was fond of everything that had an air of decision. The sharp answers and courtesies of M. Coupe had pleased him, and earned him the decoration of the *Légion d'Honneur*.

I put myself on the best terms with this new chief since I was in an element that suited me with no tedious guard to mount; a great deal of instruction to draw from a branch which had offered me only very incomplete opportunities to study it thoroughly and a position of authority in our struggles against naval officers.

The Director of Artillery of Antwerp, was in charge of implementing all that concerned the armament of the squadron, except the forging of the guns, supplying the vessels the artillery equipment and repairing it when it needed it. In fact, overall a great and interesting activity in which I regretted not having participated earlier. I count my stay in Antwerp as the most instructive time in my short military career.

During this time, I had to fulfil the mission of having all the powder of the Scheldt squadron stored in a powder magazine near Ghent, since it was considered inadvisable for its condition that it spent the winter in the basins of Antwerp. On this occasion I can give an idea of the abuses that take place in large administrations of great men who are, moreover, very honourable.

A fixed sum of money was allocated for the movement of a certain number of barrels of powder due to a certain number of horses being required for a certain number of days for its transportation. Ordinarily there was a saving over this number of days, and this saving entered into the pocket of the artillery officer in charge of the store. Of course, the officer still inscribed on the expense statements that he provided the normal number and not the real number of days of horse hire. I kept conscientiously to the real number so as not to profit from the abuse and my operation was less expensive than that of previous years, to the satisfaction of my chief, but not to that of my peers, who thought I was spoiling the job for them when their turn came for the duty.

Antwerp did not offer me the distractions of society that Boulogne had offered me. The French were not loved by the inhabitants, who closed their *salons* to emphasise their sentiments. It was necessary to be content with those entertainments offered by the authorities, which were not appealing, or to live a secluded existence. I satisfied myself in the company of M. and Mme Coupe. *Madame* was a kind and friendly woman and *Monsieur* had a slightly eccentric frame of mind which amused me very much.

Besides this personal contact Antwerp offered so many immense works in which I could find a real interest when we were not busy elsewhere. I saw Spanish prisoners of war dig one of the two docks intended to receive the squadron of the Scheldt during the winter. I also saw the construction of extensive fortifications, the purpose of which was to cover the vast construction sites of the navy.

I had resigned myself to spending the rest of my days in Antwerp when news of the disasters that had befallen the retreating French Army in Russia came to our notice and this intelligence was quickly followed by the order, arriving towards the end of winter, in 1813, to make available to the Minister of War all the troops of the Marine Artillery. These troops were to collect at Mayence and it was in the early days of February, 1813, that the detachments of artillery were withdrawn from the squadron and disembarked to direct them to that city.

GERMANY & EASTERN FRANCE
THE WAR OF LIBERATION 1813-14

English Miles

50 0 50 100

DENMARK

Holstein

Lübeck Lützow
Hamburg Meck
Lüneburg
Bremen Göhr R. Elbe

Hanover Brande
Magdeburg

Amsterdam

The Hague Münster Halberstadt

Wesel Brau
Westphalia Kitheln
Hartz Halle
Merseburg

Ghent Antwerp Düsseldorf
Cologne R. Rhine Erfurt
Eisenach Jena
Brussels Weizlar Giessen Coburg Hof

Lille Tournay Liege Coblenz Ehrenbreitstein
Mons Namur Ladnstein
Frankfort Hanau

Amiens Mezieres Treves Mainz Main

Beauvais Laon Kaiserslautern Mannheim Bavar
Compiegne Soissons Rheims Chalons Verdun
Pontoise Chateau Chatillon Metz c
Thierry Champaubert Commercy Strasbourg Würtemberg
Versailles Meaux Vauchamps
Paris Lafere Champenoise Nancy
Essonnes Melun Sezanne Vitry Mary
Fontheiry Nogent Arcis S.Aube Ligny
Etampes Mery Brienne Joinville
Fontainebleau Brau LaRothiere Chaumont
Montereau Troyes Bar
Orleans Auxerre Chatillon Langres Colmar R. Main

Dijon R. Saône Schaffhausen

Besancon Basel

THE NEIGHBOURHOOD OF PARIS

Pontoise SWISS
Conflans Montmorency CONFEDERATION
Argenteuil Denis
Poissy S.Ouen Aubervilliers Geneva
von Laye Montmartre
Marly Belleville
Malmaison Paris Chelles
Surennes Montreuil Lagny
Trianon Ivry Nogent
S.Cyr Sceaux Chateau de Vincennes
Versailles Vaudin
Vicy
Sceaux

Villeneuve S.Georges

KINGDOM OF IT

Niemen

Königsberg

Danzig Elbing East

West Marienburg P r u s s i a Lyk

Marienwerder Grodno

Swedish

omerania Graudenz

Pomerania R Stettin Stargard U Thorn

urg Oder Bromberg

randenburg S Plock

Berlin Küstrin Gnesen Warsaw Bre

Spandau Frankfort Posen R. Vistula

Blankenfeld

Jüterbog W A R S A W

Luckau Sprembg Sagan Kalisch Pilica Lublin

Hoyerswerda Oels

Massen Olgau Sandomir

Spremberg Bunzlau

Neustadt Breslau Sagan

Königstein Reichenbach S i l e s i a

Oder Cracow G a l i c i a

R. Elbe Prague

B o h e m i a R. Oder

Pilsen

Schweidnitz

A U S T R I A N   E M P I R E

Vienna

R. Elster From Halle R. Parthe Taucha

R. Luppe Möckern Eutritsch Schönfeld To Wurzen

From Merseburg Gohlis Pfaffendf Paunsdorf

Lindenau LEIPZIG Stünz

Connewitz Stötteritz

Markranstadt Lösnig Holzhausen

Dölitz Probstheida

Liebertwolkwitz

Markkleeberg Gautzsch To Dresden

Lützen Wachau

Y P r o v i n c e s Kaja

R. Elster R. Pleisse THE NEIGHBOURHOOD

Kitzsch OF

Görschen LEIPZIG

Chapter Six

The March to War: Lützen

Staying in Antwerp when my regiment was marching on the enemy would have meant for me the giving up of the promise of both laurels and promotion. It was impossible to remain in this place, and resisting all the representations of M. Coupe, who wished to keep me with him, I signed my name on the roll of the troop which was leaving. I was pleased that this departure was not delayed for two or three days afterwards, for M. Coupe had obtained from the Naval Ministry an order to compel me to stay in Antwerp, but by the time it arrived the 'bird had flown the coop'!

My father, whom I did not consult on the matter, did not see with the same eye or the same hope as myself the glory of French arms and much preferred for me to be engaged in a scholarly service filled with security rather than the adventurous pursuits in which I was about to risk life and limb. He therefore, as is understandable, viewed my escapade very badly.

Such considerations did not enter my head and it was as a future hero that I entered the town of Mayence on February 23rd 1813. What I saw there served to reduce somewhat my dreams of glory. These men we met were the first remnants of the retreat from Russia, isolated officers and soldiers arriving covered in dilapidated clothes and several of them mutilated by frostbite. Such remained, however, the confidence in the person and fortune of Napoleon that it did not come into the minds of any of those conscripts who were to be led to the slaughter, and

Battle of LUTZEN.
May 2nd. 1813.
English Miles.

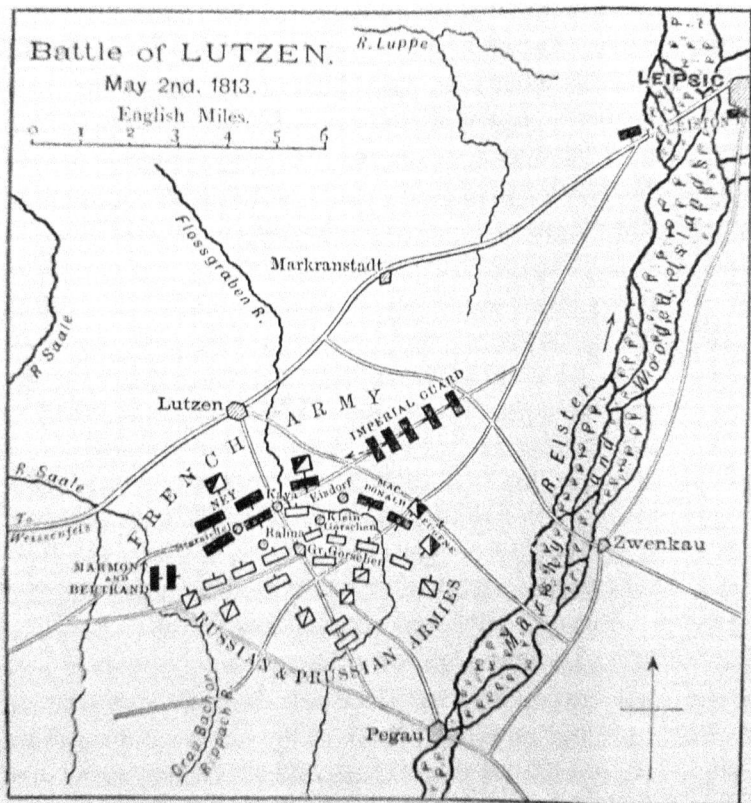

R. Luppe

LEIPSIC

Markranstadt

Flossgraben R.

R. Saale

R. Saale

To Weissenfels

Lutzen

FRENCH   ARMY

IMPERIAL GUARD

NEY   Kaya   Eisdorf

MAC DONALD

Klein Gorschen

Rahna

Gr. Gorschen

MARMON AND BERTRAND

PRUSSIAN & PRUSSIAN ARMIES

Gros Bach or Rippach R.

Pegau

R. Elster

Zwenkau

had before their eyes a so discouraging a spectacle, to doubt that the future held anything for them but victories.

Marshal Kellermann was then in command at Mayence. He did not let us enter that city, but made us fall back to Kreutznach, where we remained quartered for about a month, awaiting the arrival of the other Marine Artillery troops coming from Brest and the other ports. At the end of this time we were reviewed and crossed the Rhine at the beginning of April, 1813, in order to be assembled in an army corps in the neighbourhood of Frankfort. This corps was the VI, commanded by the Marshal, Duke of Raguse, that is to say Marmont. It consisted of two divisions: The 1st, of which my regiment was a part, was commanded by General Compans; the second was under General Bonnet. The army corps had a total of about 16,000 men, including about 14,000 troops of the Marine Artillery.

At that time, on April 16th 1813, I was appointed to the rank of captain. I therefore entered the field at the head of a company, having for lieutenants two young officers who had just left the school of St Cyr. In spite of our title of artillerymen we were obliged to serve only as infantry and as we completed our long-neglected cadres the gaps were temporarily filled, for the time of our service on land, in part by infantry officers. I had for a *chef de battalion* an excellent man, named Préville though he was not very military in his background for he had made his previous campaigns in Paris as officer in charge of recruiting the army.

It was in the neighbourhood of Naumburg, a town situated on the road from Frankfort to Leipzig, that our first bivouac was made. It signalled the approach of the enemy, and it was not without some emotion that I first saw two leagues from there at Weissenfels, the traces of the bivouac of the Russian advance guard which had retired on our approach. There were some corpses left in the area following an action which had taken place between the Russian division commanded by Winzingerode and Souham's division of the French III Corps, an affair of ill omen as it transpired, for Marshal Bessières, commanding the cavalry of the Imperial Guard and close friend of Napoleon,

BATTLE OF LÜTZEN

had been killed there by a stray ball which had ricocheted off a wall and struck him in the chest.

The next day, 2nd May 1813, the army began to move on Leipzig, our corps forming the rear guard; but it was found that the enemy, instead of concentrating around Leipzig as was originally supposed made a diversion on the right of the army which it then sought to turn. The order was immediately sent to the VI Corps to march across the fields at the *'pas de course'* (200-250 paces per minute) on the right, where the enemy's General in Chief, Wittgenstein, had assembled a formidable artillery and all his cavalry, to cut off the retreat of the French, the main body of which had been stopped at Lützen by the enemy forces.

Thus, we found ourselves, the VI Corps, exposed to a powerful attack in order to protect the rest of the army and were obliged to maintain a firm footing for about four hours against seven cavalry charges plus a constant hail of balls and grapeshot which decimated us. We had neither artillery nor cavalry to support us, the artillery having been concentrated at the centre of the army, and the cavalry, destroyed in the retreat from Russia, having not yet been re-organised.

I do not conceal the fact that the first limb that I saw carried away by a cannon ball made a very disagreeable impression on me, and that, in spite of all my warlike ardour, I should have been more at ease at a respectable distance from the enemy's cannon. I nevertheless succeeded in overcoming this first emotion; there was, moreover, no means of changing the situation and as one does to everything, the continual spectacle of men struck by my side whose brains more than once splattered upon me, the thunderous roll of hundreds of cannon, the whistling of projectiles, the hurrahs of the cavalry charges, the sound of musketry, the cries of the wounded, all of this caused a kind of deafness and excitement such that no one thought of his own preservation.

Weakened by such a disproportionate struggle, I saw the moment when we were going to be forced to retreat or turned and routed by superior forces; then, fortunately the corps of General Bertrand arrived from a distant position and, having force marched to our aid, came to support our threatened right and made the enemy withdraw. The advantage also remained to the French at Lützen, the centre of the army, so that, the battle won, we had a much-needed respite for us to re-organise. I found myself very fortunate to be left only with a contusion on the back of my neck caused by a bullet of grape-shot hitting the padded collar of my great-coat. The blow had violently thrown me face first into the ground, and as I got up, I had a foretaste of my death by finding my lieutenant had placed himself at the head of my company, convinced that I had been killed.

The Battle of Lützen was won gloriously by an army of young conscripts, but the absence of cavalry rendered the results null and void. Fearing the numerous cavalry which the enemy had, we were obliged to pass the night formed in squares on the very field of battle. It was well that we did, because at 10 o'clock in the evening and in deep darkness, we suddenly heard the trampling of horses, the trumpet sounding the charge and we were surrounded by the enemy's cavalry, disconcerted to find us on our guard. The surprise was lost and after galloping around the squares two or three times, unloading their pistols, they were forced to withdraw, leaving many victims from the fire of our musketry.

We were opposed in this skirmish to a body of volunteer cavalry organised in Berlin, young people of good family, excellently equipped, several came to fall in the midst of our squares.

The experience of a great battle taught me how passive the role of a subaltern officer is; enclosed in a line he often has only the merit of patience, rarely that of active courage, at this lowest price he can be a hero. He ordinarily knew neither the places nor the strength of the armies, nor their general position, nor the object of the operations and he was reduced to admiring himself afterwards for exploits of which he did not suspect in the exaggerated bulletins, while the honest *bourgeois* reading the gazette with his feet on the fire-dog knows a thousand times better than himself what he has done.

From Lützen the army moved on Dresden in pursuit of the

Russo-Prussian Army, which withdrew in very good order guarded by its cavalry; and in Dresden the advanced guard was even obliged to cannonade for a whole day with the Russians, who had blown up the beautiful bridge arch over the Elbe.

In Dresden from 10th–12th May we took a much-needed rest, for we must not forget that we were at the beginning of the life of camps and battles, and this beginning had been as abrupt as it was rude. Besides the blows of the enemy we had the fatigue of incessant marches and, above all, the deprivation of any regular distribution of provisions, plus nights spent under the stars.

CHAPTER SEVEN

The Battle of Bautzen

Our inaction did not last long, and on the 12th of May we were marching on the road to Bautzen and crossing the hot and devastated streets of the small town of Bischofswerda, burnt down in the fighting of the advanced guard. On the 13th we arrived in sight of Bautzen; a pretty town situated on the Spree at the bottom of a valley crowned by heights. The view that was offered to us was magnificent and such that in a man's life one rarely encounters them. The view embraced, on either side of the valley, two armies established in the presence of one another and each amounting to nearly one hundred thousand men.

As far as the eye could see there were shining weapons and columns of dust raised by the corps taking their positions. The respective outposts were almost in contact, separated by a narrow and shallow stream. Close by, the agitation of this united multitude, horses, wagons going in all directions, foragers leaving and others returning laden with the remains of neighbouring villages, real or false alerts caused by the proximity of the enemy and which made us take up arms. In a word, all this hubbub repeated for an extent of nearly three leagues, was a deafening spectacle.

The Russo-Prussian Army had therefore stopped at Bautzen, a town it occupied and fortified, deploying itself on the right bank of the Spree and offering us battle. Our inaction could not last long, for the concentration of so many men in a narrow area of land led to a scarcity of food and forced the soldiers to spread

BAUTZEN

Dobeschau Priewitz

Ober
Kayna

Strehla

Marshal Macdonald

Gorubnitz
Falkenberg

Baroswitz

Mehlthiuer

Jenkwitz

Pielitz

Weissig

Kubschütz

Hochkirch

BATTLE
OF
BAUTZEN
20 & 21 May 1813.

French ▬▬▬   Allies ▬▬▬
Cavalry ▬◄   Infantry ▬◄   Artillery ▬◄

SCALE
Military Steps 24 feet each

English Miles

Dallwitz

Malsitz
Kymmschatza

Hohe
Berg

Bautzen

Oberanbaus

Zischelwitz

Plasckewitz

Malschwitz

Basankwitz

Jenkwitz

Blucker

Litten

Kl. Bautzen

Deutly

Lubau

Wurschen

Markind

Dratitz

Glenna

Victor

Reguey

Belgern

Rackel

Baruth

Lohau

Triessnitz

Kurschen

Dubrauke

W.&.A.K.Johnston Edin.

abroad for marauding, where they were exposed to being taken by the Cossacks, which was the case for many.

At dawn on the 20th May, Napoleon travelled the line with his staff to reconnoitre the position of the enemy which was the presage of the battle. This would be a battle planned and meditated upon for several days and not improvised, as was that of Lützen. Thus, so many men, still very full of life, were to be corpses in a few hours, but none of them appeared to be concerned with this thought. Each believed themselves to have a good chance in this lottery of human lives. Enthusiasm for the Emperor and assured victory. That was all that came into the mind of the French soldier; a soldier of action, little a thinker of his own nature, born for success, which is not made for serious or philosophical ideas, and with which one can undertake everything, but at the expense of success.

Our corps occupied the centre of the line in the area of the town of Bautzen. A cannonade engaged on the extreme left, by a corps sent to turn the enemy, began the action. We had the mission to seize Bautzen and for that purpose we had to march under the fire of a formidable battery which defended the approaches, and which we were obliged to take from the rear, after having forded the Spree. This manoeuvre succeeded, but it cost us many men.

The enemy battery turned was evacuated and we found ourselves formed in battle on the left of the town, which was occupied without much trouble. I cannot help mentioning here a manoeuvre of a different kind by our colonel. He had distributed clothing effects to the troops before the battle, but in an incomplete way, presuming that death would come to his aid to justify or to confuse its delivery statements, to his advantage in all cases. He was right, materially speaking, and this reminds me that one of my distractions while the bullets decimated my company was to take from the dead the objects which were missing from the living.

After five hours of fighting and after having undergone several cavalry charges, we took a position at night before the en-

Battle of Bautzen

emy's army, which had only retreated on a second line, chosen and fortified in advance, so the job was only half done and we had the certainty of starting the dance again the next day.

It was necessary that military honour alone should sustain the soldiers, for the day had passed without eating anything but a few miserable potatoes plundered the day before and there was no question of renewing the provision under the fire of the enemy army.

The next day, May 21st, Napoleon arrived at daybreak, without a staff, dismounting from his horse in front of our regiment and pointing his telescope at the enemy's corps. I saw him speak to General Compans, whose ear he tweaked, the usual sign of his satisfaction.

★★★★★★

Here is a trait of the Emperor that we reproduce as we have collected from the mouth of the author. 'In reviewing his troops, the Emperor sometimes took pleasure in surprising his officers with unannounced questions. If one answered promptly, and especially with assurance and decision, the answers were agreed upon, whatever they were; but the officer who had the misfortune to hesitate, even for a moment, whatever his merit, was lost without return in his papers.'—Charles Rieu.

★★★★★★

Before us was an enormous Russian (artillery) battery of heavy calibre, duly fortified, placed the day before, at the centre of the line. Our corps had the assignment of making a false attack in front of it and holding it while the real attack would take place on the left by Marshal Ney's Corps. This explains why, for our part, the whole of the day passed passively receiving cannon balls with our weapons on our arms. (*'L'arme au bras'* a comfortable position to carry the musket, resting in the crook of the arm, on the lock). As at Lützen our loss was great; a battery of howitzers above all preoccupied us; the shells rained in the middle of our squares, we were obliged to lie down to wait for the moment when the projectile burst. More than once, placed in the line of fire of a ball I avoided the blow by a sideways movement.

I cannot forget in this bloody butchery two incidents which made a particular impression. I saw an old soldier whose thigh had just been struck by a cannon ball and he coolly cut off the shreds of flesh which still held the limb and lit his pipe, which he smoked while shouting '*Vive l'Empereur*'. A young and charming lieutenant who had arrived a few days before from the school of St Cyr, and belonging to a good family, wanted, despite warnings to the contrary, to leave the square to see what was going on more easily; he was instantly hit with a shell burst that tore his arm, a mortal wound. That confirmed in me the superstition of never changing my official post before the enemy, or my tour of duty, believing thus to avoid unnecessary and regrettable injuries.

The first day was named the Battle of Bautzen and the second was called the Battle of Wurschen, a small town situated behind the enemy's entrenched camp, and whose capture by Marshal Ney decided the victory. This 'victory' was not decisive due to the want of cavalry, for the enemy, leaving only their dead, retreated in good order without losing any prisoners or artillery. In any case, it was a fine moment for us when we saw those cannon which persecuted us flee, and we occupied the entrenched camp abandoned by the enemy.

It must be added that on that day at least we had the feeling that we had understood the battle well, for the position of each army, as in an amphitheatre, made it easy to see and grasp the whole and the result of the manoeuvres. The Emperor was almost constantly placed behind our corps and remarked that we had to suffer a lot; it must be confessed that ambition and egoism sometimes rejoiced at these losses and that it was not always out of sheer commiseration that young officers like myself inquired carefully after the affair of the health of their superiors.

CHAPTER EIGHT

The Pursuit

The 22nd of May saw us early in the tracks of the enemy; the VI Corps, not being in the vanguard we had only to march and not to fight, we were on the right of the army, near the mountains of Bohemia and having before us Wittgenstein, withdrawing on Breslau. Thus, we arrived at Jauer, near Schweidnitz, at a distance of about 40 leagues from Bautzen, on the 29th of May.

I suffered greatly on this occasion from the deprivation of sleep; I was also suffering from the visit of a new acquaintance, vermin, which I caught from the straw of the bivouacs where the Russians had preceded us. I often dreamed while marching and even fell asleep. The soldiers were also falling asleep, and often fell, losing their grips on their muskets. The halt at night, a late halt, meant that one rested very little, with the time divided between the duties of the guard and the obligation to find food and shelter.

A company commander was also anxious to see his soldiers, for tired or starving, scattering on the way, he arrived at the bivouac with only half or a quarter of the company. Even then, it was necessary to officially send what remained of the troops to plunder wood, straw and provisions in the neighbouring villages. Then, with the materials thus assembled, we had to prepare a shelter, that is to say, a kind of roof, sufficient at least, to cover the head of the soldier lying on the straw. Then it was necessary to cook the food, assuming that there was firewood and food to be cooked, which did not always happen. Finally, after a frugal meal we took a late rest, soon interrupted, at dawn, by the drum which called the troops to remain under arms while reconnoitring cavalry would observe the position of the enemy.

The provost and outpost guards were provided by whole companies, and it was a service that was dictated much more by the instinct of one's own safety than by regulations ignored by superior officers themselves. For example, I do not recall ever having given or received a password during the whole campaign.

The lack of regular distributions essentially relaxed the rules of discipline; there was formed in the rear of the army bodies of marauders much more feared by the unfortunate inhabitants than the army itself. The officers, while deploring the marauding, could only live by taking part in the plunder of their soldiers. We understood that this changed the relations between the chief and the subordinate, and that, if there was less severity than in the life of the garrison, there was, on the other hand, more intimacy.

A company became a sort of family where one helped another out of benevolence more than by duty, and nothing was more unfortunate sometimes than a staff officer without a troop. I have not, for my part, preserved a disagreeable memory in this way of being one against the others, although I have never been completely separated from a harshness which was in my bearing.

In general, there is a great difference between the regulatory theory and the serious practice of military service in the field. In garrison life it is necessary to occupy the soldier's leisure and to break him to the discipline by a thousand meticulous duties which are unlearned by war, in which everything takes on the new form dictated by circumstances and imperious necessity. It is another type of school, but an intelligent one that reaches its goal by the shortest route and whose lessons are etched forever in the memory.

We seem disposed, at the present time, to bring the regime of peace and war more in harmony. We feel the need to simplify a little the complications of the service, of making the uniform less embarrassing and less burdened with useless superfluities and finally to prune a good number of parade ground manoeu-

Uniform of the Marine Artillery
with bicorne and greatcoat

vres and to limit oneself to what is practised before the enemy. What I saw in 1813 is well suited to justify such simplifications, an army composed largely of rough conscripts behaved in line with the *sang-froid* and aplomb of old soldiers.

We stopped in front of Jauer for three or four days, to await the conclusion of an armistice which was being negotiated at Neumarck, in the neighbourhood of Breslau, and signed on the 4th of June 1813. We then withdrew to Bunzlau, a city in Silesia, and not without satisfaction, for there was the prospect of a peace which would enable us to display our laurels in France.

CHAPTER NINE

The Armistice

The Compans' division, of which I was a member, was quartered during the armistice near Bunzlau. My regiment occupied a village called Gnadenberg, two leagues from that city. This village was a creation and a current establishment of Moravian brothers. My company was established in an adjoining village, the inhabitants of which had fled and where only a few old people remained. In the town of Bunzlau the civilian part of the population had emigrated in fear or hatred of the French.

The armistice was rightly regarded by those who mingled with politics as a great fault on the Emperor's part. The Allies had no other aim than to reorganise and strengthen themselves by attracting Austria into the contest, who had hitherto been neutral, and whose sword was destined to tip the balance on their side. The French Army, little initiated into the secrets of diplomacy, greeted the truce with pleasure, for she was tired.

Our Marshal, Marmont, himself appeared a little tired of war, he had courage, but little happiness and later his capitulation of Paris in 1814 proved that he still preferred peace than to wage war for his Emperor. I have rarely seen a figure gloomier than his. A beard and very black hair contributed to this effect and finally his lip perpetually ignored a smile. One could not, however, contest his bravery. He had, like Compans and Pelleport, an imperturbable coolness in the midst of the most terrible fire, and none of them betrayed the slightest emotion.

Marmont had often been wounded in the war, when he as-

MARSHAL MARMONT

GENERAL PELLEPORT

GENERAL COMPANS

COLONEL EMOND

sumed command of our corps, he still had his arm in a sling after a shell burst had wounded him at Salamanca whilst serving in the Army of Spain. But military courage alone is not enough for general officers. They must also be able to inspire the soldier by heroic words and by an air of assurance and cheerfulness. This is what the Duke of Raguse (Marmont) did not do, for this reason he was viewed with complete indifference by his men.

General Pelleport was a man of great merit. He had commanded our brigade since the approach to Dresden. He has, since the peace was made, been in great favour as Lieutenant-General, having been on the infantry steering committee and has been one of the best inspectors of this branch. Perfectly instructed himself, he insisted on the personal instruction of his subordinates. He contrasted with our colonel, usually invisible (without being enchanted to make an appearance!) and routinely grumbling without justifiable reason.

General Pelleport often gave me marks of interest, of which I keep a precious memory, for I feel that flattery, which is not my weakness, had no part in it. Full of humanity towards the victims of war, he had the urbanity of a very well-mannered man, without ever departing from the difficult task of ensuring regularity of the service. It was difficult not to admire him, and one could not admire him without loving him at the same time.

As for our major, the war only added to his defects. He received, at the beginning of the campaign, some praise for an expedition from which he had done well so that his natural pride had increased to the highest level and his usual brutality turned into ferocity. I heard him one day, at the end of a tiring march, give orders to a non-commissioned officer to administer blows with a ramrod to a soldier who had been left behind, and, as the NCO was executing this outrageous act of severity reluctantly, I saw the major get off his horse, seize the ramrod of a gun, and himself beat with a hard rod a poor devil exhausted with fatigue. All this in the presence of a whole regiment, who thought that their chief deserved much more fury than his victim, but discipline required a sad silence.

My farmer's cottage, near Gnadenberg, seemed to me a palace after five or six weeks of bivouacking under the stars, and the straw made me the most comfortable of beds. I lodged there with my lieutenant, and we had in common the enjoyment of a dairy cow, dispersed in the park of the division. I also enjoyed a small mare which one of my soldiers had procured for me and whose title to property was, alas, justified only by the law of war, and by the impossibility of making, as I should have liked, the return to the true owner of a token which I had not ordered, and from which I did not profit from other than with reluctance. On the march, this horse carried my modest valise and those of my officers. I did not mount it. In the cantonments I used it to run errands in the vicinity, especially in Bunzlau, where the officers of the army corps met in a smoking house to drink beer, smoke tobacco and talk politics.

The town of Gnadenberg was not entirely without inhabitants, for only the luminaries had left it. It consisted of a quadrangle of very clean buildings, built on a uniform plan, in the centre was the church. The locals we met were good, honest and helpful. When later on, returning from captivity in Russia, we crossed, in rags, the village which we had occupied as victors, these same people recognised us, in spite of our misery, and we were showered with signs of affection and offers of service, which is to their credit and a little of our own, for it proved that we had not abused victory when the scales tilted in our favour.

The armistice was put to good use to manoeuvre the division from time to time in the cornfields, which were trodden underfoot without mercy; we were in a vanquished country. The general, not content with the regulation exercises, added some manoeuvres of his own. Needless to say, the enemy never had the pleasure of seeing one executed, for the regulation manoeuvres themselves were reduced to the simplest form when they were used seriously. In any case, it was interesting enough for me to be exercised in this manner in the company of seven or eight thousand men, a rare occurrence in the garrison exercises.

In one of these manoeuvres I found myself at the head of

a platoon, on which was to be deployed the whole division. I thought I was sure of my business, when an unfortunate adjutant, thinking himself in the battalion school, came to stop the platoon at the battalion's head, whereas it was necessary to lead it to the head of the division, a few hundred paces further on. Without realising the purpose, I believed that this adjutant acted by order of a superior and I halted. But a storm, in the form of an *aide-de-camp* of the *général de division* came upon me and made me notice my blunder.

Then came the general himself in a state of concentrated fury; I thought he would pierce me with his sword, and, without listening to my justification, he ordered me, somewhat vaguely it is true, to be arrested after the exercise. It was understood that there was an outburst of the moment which would soon be forgotten and afterwards I never heard a word spoken of these events. I do not know whether Compans, who just died in 1845, bequeathed me in his will as a proof of his memory of me.

During the armistice there was a distribution of the *Legion d'Honneur*, in which I was not included at all. I experienced a great disappointment, because I saw more than one officer decorated whose merit was dubious, but the colonel presented the list of proposals and an unfair bias was to be expected because of this. The good Monsieur Préville, my *chef de battalion*, was not an accomplice to this breach of regulations because he showed me all his grief. This dear colonel himself received a reward no less gracious for us than for him; he was appointed *général de brigade* and left us. *Bon Voyage!* I learned afterwards that he had been taken prisoner at Dresden with Marshal Gouvion St Cyr's corps, and that he died during his captivity.

At this time, the number of officers of the regiment, having been greatly decimated by the war, was complemented by infantry officers drawn from the Army of Spain. These gentlemen, in general had purses much better furnished than ours were, which was attributed in part to certain exactions towards the inhabitants of the country in which they had lately been serving. This extraordinary wealth was very common among the officers formerly of the Army of Spain and some of them even naively regretted this resource, which was wanting now they were members of the Army of Germany. I hasten to say in honour of my compatriots, that one of them was an exception; he was a Genevan and his name was Ramu. His rank was that of Captain, and he was placed precisely in my battalion. It is easy to understand that I soon became acquainted with him. I did it all the more willingly as Ramu, without having exactly received a liberal education, had judgement, experience, courage and a charming character.

The armistice had been prolonged in the hope of a pacification, but this hope was deceived and it was soon discovered that the hostilities were about to recommence, when the Emperor brought forward the celebration of his birthday to the 10th of August, the ordinary date of which was the 15th of that month.

That day, Marshal Marmont, with his baton in his hand, standing like the statue of Festin de Pierre, and no less grave and sombre than this monument, reviewed our *corps d'armée*. Then, in the church of Gnadenberg, there was a meal for all the officers of the division where quite inflated toasts were officially proposed to the Emperor and his family. Our general, Pelleport, who was not a talkative man, was even less so than usual because he proposed without comment the health of the little King of Rome, like a soldier who executes his orders. He would have carried, with the same coolness, the health of the Pope, had the Pope been in his place, so he would regulate matters.

The armistice expired on 16th August 1813, after two and a half months and our corps left their cantonments to resume the bivouac.

CHAPTER TEN

The Battle of Dresden & After

The Prussian Field Marshal, Blücher began hostilities on the Bober, a river which passes through Bunzlau. His attack took place at Löwenberg, above Bunzlau. The Emperor arrived from Dresden with his Guard and repulsed Blücher, while we were manoeuvring on his left to cover Bunzlau.

But on the 23rd August the news arrived of the invasion of Saxony by another Allied army, which included forces furnished by Austria, which had thus renounced its neutrality. The attack took place through the mountains of Bohemia upon Dresden. This news decided the Emperor to go suddenly, by forced marches, with his Guard on the attack point, leaving our army corps the order to follow it. MacDonald, the Duke of Tarentum, remained in Silesia to contain Blücher.

In going to this new destination, we slept on the battlefield at Bautzen, still covered with the debris of the last battle. We had left it victorious, we returned with less hope, but not discouraged. From Bunzlau to Dresden is about 40 leagues, which we covered in three days in a continuous and pouring rain and almost without eating. A few hours of rest were taken during the night, we slept in a furrow where one's body remained half-awake in the water.

How often I have thought of the numerous precautions that one takes at home to preserve oneself from a cold wind, which one does not always avoid. I could not, on later reflection, prevent myself from seeing a perfect justification of the hydropathic medi-

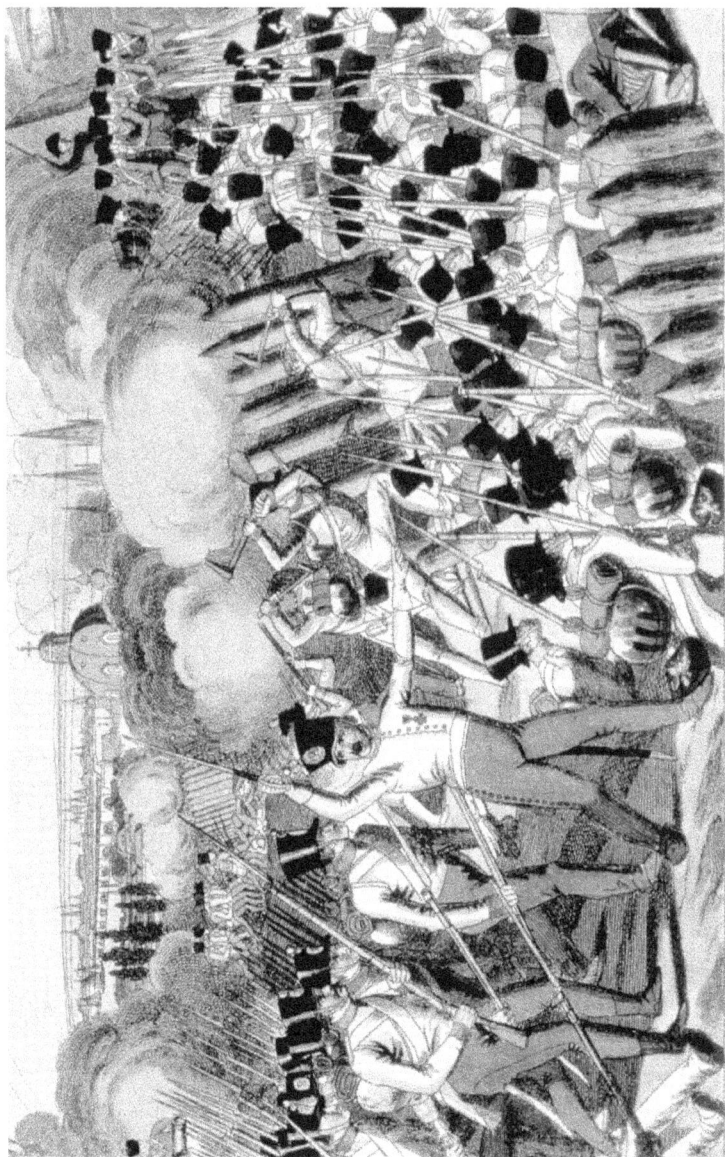

Battle of Dresden

cal system in this life so wet, so contrary to the rules of hygiene, and yet which left me in good health. It must be admitted, however, that more than one poor soldier, falling exhausted on the road, would have pleaded in favour of the system. Yet there was no complaint! They were marching into the fire with the Emperor. This made the men overcome every obstacle in their way.

We reached Dresden on 26th of August. There had been fighting on the other side of the Elbe since the morning and we could hear the sound of cannon and musketry in the distance. We found a momentary shelter in the suburb, where we were stationed, wet to the bone, throughout the whole day. The next day, the second day of the Battle of Dresden, it was only in the afternoon that our corps was ordered to cross the town to the battlefield by the Dippoldiswalde gate. The affair was then almost finished; we were left to receive a few stray balls.

To compensate us we had the spectacle of the return to Dresden of the Emperor, all dripping with water, and that of a column of Austrian prisoners, with a battery, also Austrian. The fierce look of these prisoners, the exaltation of the Frenchmen who escorted them, the enthusiasm of the population of Dresden, all made a most dramatic contrast which I will never forget. Furthermore, after all these emotions, and to bring them to a climax, they took care to make us pass before a redoubt which had been taken, retaken and then again attacked during the day and the ditches of which were literally filled with the corpses of Hungarian Grenadiers whose faces still bore the imprint of the desperate rage with which they had conducted the assault.

We bivouacked during the night of the 27th to the 28th of August, in the water and on the field of battle. On the morning of the 28th, the rain gave way to the most beautiful sun. The enemy had pulled out overnight and we were thrown into the pursuit in the mountain passes of Bohemia. The Emperor was to accompany us, but being indisposed, he contented himself with seeing us pass before him, with his hands behind his back on the side of the road, in front of his tent and a huge brazier he could be seen as a monumental figure, the big boots, the little

NAPOLEON STANDING ALONE

hat, the grey frock coat, nothing was wanting, it was the exact resemblance of his portrait or statue.

We were made to climb the mountains of Bohemia by the valley of Dippoldiswalde pushing before us the enemy's rearguard, commanded by Generals Colloredo and Chasteler and obliged them to abandon carriages, caissons and ammunition, in dreadful paths soaked by rain.

Here began for us a war of detail, more interesting and no less dangerous than war in open country, for there was between the two wars all the difference between active courage and purely passive courage. The two divisions which comprised the army corps alternated between them to march in the vanguard. Almost always, morning and evening, there was an engagement either to occupy the position at night or to leave it. Moreover, if in his march the enemy found an advantageous position, he contested it to delay the pursuit. Despite this, it was easy to recognise the confusion in which the lost battle had placed the Austrian Army, for the stragglers, hungry and tired, let themselves be picked up in large numbers and without resistance by our soldiers, as untrained as themselves but much more alert and moreover buoyed up by success.

On the 29th August there was a rather lively engagement, in which we were obliged, with the bayonet, to flush out the enemy who occupied the edge of a wood, from which they troubled our flanks. Their cannon, placed on a neighbouring height, killed a few men by firing in the thick of the thicket where we were. Since it was difficult to distinguish anything clearly in a very dark wood, one of our officers, separated from his company, travelled for a time with the Austrians, whom he mistook for Frenchmen. Let us imagine his confusion when he recognised his error! The enemy, who had, fortunately, to think of their own safety, allowed him time, thanks to the trees, to make a prudent retreat!

On the 30th August, the enemy's rear-guard, having reached the highest point of the valley, wished to hold out some time before descending into the valley of Toeplitz where the bulk of

Battle of Dresden

the Austrians were concentrated.

The battalion to which I belonged, with a battalion of *voltigeurs* attached was charged with attacking a height occupied by skirmishers and mountain guns. The attack, which succeeded and where more than one ball whistled in our ears, did us honour, for we had for our witness' the rest of the corps, halted at the foot of the height. I had occasion to remark then, on the courage of my compatriot, Ramu. He led by his determination, a new *chef de battalion* who had been given to us, an infantry officer more talkative and presumptuous than brave on this occasion. My company and that of Ramu, having been launched forward to skirmish, I could see at close quarters how courageous and bold was my compatriot.

We had, in this little action, the curious spectacle of an officer of *voltigeurs,* with an impressive moustache, whose courage had failed him and whose own soldiers were provoking, by overwhelming him with insults to advance into the fire. Later perhaps, this same officer will have made the walls of a garrison *café* resound with the sound of his brave exploits performed on that day. This is often how it happens with these opponents of peace.

The next day, the 31st of August, there was no forward movement, but a continual firing in the woods and in the evening, orders came to light great fires and to retreat during the night. The cause of this change was soon known, it was the defeat of General Vandamme at Culm, on our left, which had taken place on the 30th August.

That night a march in a wooded mountain was painful, the fate of the wounded was especially sad. We were obliged to have them carried by the soldiers and from drudgery, bumping, sometimes tumbling and almost abandoned by negligence or ill will, these unfortunates had much to suffer. The enemy, however, did not trouble us and we had only a few cavalry scouts and a few skirmishers in our rear.

Our return to Dresden was sad compared to the departure. It was no longer a question of setbacks. On the 23rd August the defeat of the Duke of Reggio (Oudinot) marching on Berlin;

The 26th, the defeat of MacDonald in Silesia; on the 30th, the defeat of Vandamme at Culm and a few days after, the defeat of Ney at Dennewitz on the road to Berlin by the Swedish-Prussian Army which had already defeated the Duke of Reggio. The storm was obviously growing over our heads, for we were surrounded by the powerful armies of the allies which were much more numerous than ours.

Blücher, the victor (he had beaten MacDonald in Silesia) advanced on the road to Dresden and our corps, returning from the frontiers of Bohemia, was ordered to follow the road to Bautzen with the Imperial Guard. The Prussian vanguard was already there. It was the second time that we were marching with the Guard and if this circumstance flattered our self-esteem it also had its disadvantages because the Guard, the most privileged corps, always took up, to the detriment of the other troops, what was best in cantonments and provisions. However, it was, all prejudice apart, an admirable thing to see in the midst of all the combats, disasters or bad weather, a corps always perfectly disciplined, marching and fighting as one man, whose soul was Napoleon.

My new battalion commander was not unkind, but cheerful and modest. He wished, in the beginning, to quarrel with me, wrongly, on some points of service. I corrected him so as to make him lose this habit and he became pleasant to me.

Our excursion on the road to Silesia was not of long duration, we left Dresden on the 3rd September and advanced beyond Görlitz pushing before us the rear-guard of Blücher, who, knowing well what he had to do to the Emperor, did not stand and retired behind the Queiss where he was left in peace and we returned to Dresden. Our return took place on the 7th September; up to the 9th we were established under the walls of this town, in a camp built with all possible elegance by the Young Guard, who had left us. We took a very necessary and very agreeable rest through the resources of a great city. But this was not of long duration, for, on the 9th September, our corps was sent in observation on the road to Torgau with all the cavalry, commanded by Murat, the King of Naples.

French Military Camp

We were destined to prevent the junction of the Silesian Army, commanded by Blücher, with that of Berlin, commanded by Bernadotte, Prince Royal of Sweden, who was thus fighting against his former compatriots. We were stationed at Grossenhain, on the right bank of the Elbe, about ten leagues from Dresden.

Our station at Grossenhain was spent in reconnaissance on the line of the Elster, which was lined by Blücher's army. I once commanded two companies detached from the battalion to support a regiment of *Chasseurs à Cheval* charged with scouting the quite woody countryside. I was put under the orders of an old cavalry general, whose name I have forgotten, and who was supervising the operation. After a while the reconnaissance seemed to be over, and my soldiers, kept long under arms, dying of fatigue and hunger, I went, together with Ramu, captain of the other company, to request the old general to liberate us by sending us back to camp.

This general, believing, or seeming to believe, that we wanted to abandon him, and his cavalrymen, to the Prussians, received us very badly, saying that he would make his report of a step which he regarded as contrary to discipline. His anger seemed ridiculous to us and we did not feel that it was any more than a threat. We knew how to deal with these capricious whiffs and we were correct, because the report of the old general is still yet to be written. What is more, ashamed probably of having forgotten us, but of course, not being able to admit it, this general bade us leave as we had requested just three minutes after his outburst. That is war. Ramu, full of candour, always liked to remind me of the old commanding general's anger and our surprise.

It was in the camp of Grossenhain that I had one of my better days. The troops were under arms when they had the pleasure of hearing me called to receive the decoration of the *Légion d'Honneur*. At the age of 25 such an award is perforce a joy and, during the first few days after I had received this medal, I admiringly glanced more than once at my buttonhole. What a happy time it is when one can be satiated on what is essentially nothing! What disenchantments I had from that time onwards! Not the least was to see this decoration that I had obtained at the risk of my life, without having asked for it, handed out since then to the intrigue and the courting of so many people who would be embarrassed to enumerate their merits.

Blücher crossed the Elbe, far away from our position, on October 3rd and this movement forced the VI Corps to re-cross the river itself at Meissen, then to move on Düben where we remained for three days, in front of this city, in the presence of the enemy outposts, from which we were separated by the River Mulde. The Emperor joined us there on the 10th October, with his Guard, but Blücher retired upon his approach and we therefore occupied Düben.

MÖCKERN

CHAPTER ELEVEN

The Battle of Leipzig

Napoleon stayed in Düben until October 15th. During this time, he directed our army corps on Leipzig, because he had learned that the Allied Forces were concentrating on this point. We found in Leipzig the corps of the Duke of Bellune (Victor, II Corps), the Duke of Castiglione (Augereau, IX Corps) and General Bertrand (IV Corps). The Emperor soon followed us there with the rest of the army. After many counter-marches around Leipzig we took up a position north of the city around the villages of Möckern and Euteritsch, having our back to the Partha and responsible for holding the army commanded by Blücher, 70,000 strong by the addition of Sacken's and Langeron's corps.

We were in position around large factories having a rather extensive view of the future battlefield: outposts of cavalry were already making a little war, not very lethal, and which did not look bad, like a play at the theatre.

The fatal day of 16th October 1813 finally appeared. We were, as I said, north of Leipzig in a position quite isolated from the rest of the army, of which we were placed on the extreme right. (See map p.178). At 9 o'clock in the morning the cannon were heard towards the centre of the army. This was the attack begun by the allies against the village of Wachau, at that time occupied by the French. We took up arms and were ranged in battle order on a height, at the foot of which were already positioned imposing enemy forces. To support us in our remote position and ex-

110

THE CHARGE OF THE BRANDENBURG HUSSARS THAT BROKE THE
MARINE ARTILLERY AT MÖCKERN

posed to a powerful attack we had only one division of Marshal Ney's army corps. The other two divisions of this corps were to form our reserve line and might have saved the day, so avoiding a defeat and captivity, but Marshal Ney had the unfortunate idea of sending them to the centre of the army, where they were of no use to anyone because of their late arrival. Thus 25,000 men and the small number of cavalry of Marshal Ney's Corps were exposed without support to the assault of nearly 70,000 men. While we took a position, Ramu found a way to tell me 'The day will be hot, if I am killed or wounded look after my shako, I have placed some papers there that are important to me.' We shall see before long the use I made of this recommendation.

Nothing was more solemn than the plan of that battle; the sun was bright and the silence profound. We were deployed in line as though for a revue, and were made to form in two ranks instead of three in order to make our front appear longer, which was a bad sign from the outset for we were in no position where an illusion would assist us.

I can still hear the flag bearer, named Mutel, ask if it would not be appropriate to put the Eagle in its case because its glare in the sun was a target for the enemy and the major answering him at the top of his voice, that on such a beautiful day the Imperial Eagle could not be too bright. I believe that Mutel and many others who stood with us that morning did not ultimately find that the day was so beautiful after all.

All too soon, the profound calm was succeeded by the roar of the cannonade and musketry. Our only artillery battery was crushed in the twinkling of an eye by the formidable artillery of the enemy and to crown it all, a caisson filled with live shells caught fire and vomited death all around as it erupted. The *tirailleurs* were forced to retreat before superior forces. Meanwhile in order to receive the approaching cavalry we were made to leave the order of battle, to form in mass by battalions, but the enemy artillery grapeshot ploughed through us only more deeply. We held on however, hoping that reserve troops would come to support us though it was a hope in vain!

However, a regiment of *Chasseurs à Cheval* made a demonstration to charge the enemy (and especially his artillery), but they had not taken twenty strides forward before they turned their bridles and left us to our unfortunate fate. We were punished more and more by the grapeshot, still in line by battalions *en masse*. No order came to us, no leaders command was heard, we had somehow been totally abandoned upon the battlefield.

This has been explained by the fact that Marshal Marmont and General Compans were wounded; I do not know if Pelleport was too, in any case, I did not see him anymore. As for my bragging little battalion commander, he was invisible! I have learned since that he had taken the pretext of a scratch upon his person to withdraw shamefully from the *mêlée*, (as did the lieutenant of my company), all without saying a word. If the major who commanded the regiment gave no sign of his presence it was because he was doubtless bewildered by the storm. At least he did not run away and later we discovered him to be a captive.

However, the Prussian infantry battalions, with the help of their artillery and our immobility, were approaching so close, that they were confused with ours; so much so that an adjutant from our regiment, named Mourgue, taking them for French, because of their blue coats, similar to ours, went off informally to warn them that they were firing badly on their companions. He was very lucky to be captured and he himself told me that fact when he was in captivity.

Our position became untenable, besides the artillery which killed us at close range, a formidable force of cavalry was waiting, motionless, twenty paces off, for the moment of our rout to rush upon us, like a tiger watching for its prey to run. The companies were disorganised, and soon the battalions, huddled in upon themselves, offered only shapeless heaps from which a few more shots were fired and over which the officers only had influence by remaining themselves and physically restraining the soldiers.

This state of affairs could not last long, the instinct of self-preservation, though badly inspired in the circumstances, finally became stronger, and we broke up as we fled. As I was carried away in the first moment by the torrent, I soon saw that all retreat was impossible for the infantryman positioned before the cavalry, and if I was to die it was at least some solace that I would see the blow coming.

I turned then, resigned to my fate, but I scarcely had time for speculation for at that moment, like a thunderbolt, a Prussian hussar struck me with his sword on my head. The blow, partly parried by my shako, made a superb gash on my forehead above the right eye, more extensive than deep, for the bone was not broken, then, meeting my right hand which was holding my sword, cut my thumb to the first joint. Thrown to the ground by the shock of the horse, I passed under the feet of a whole squadron, whose horses trampled over my body without touching me. Then I was on the point of being crushed by a battery of artillery whose wheels brushed my head as it passed. All this happened in less time than it takes one to read this short description, that is to say, two or three seconds, because in war the 'dead are going fast', as the ballad says.

I escaped from the scene of carnage only to fall prey in the less dramatic one of looting, whose actors were savage Cossacks following in the tracks of the fighters. Wounded and still lying on the ground, my purse, my watch, my epaulettes were nimbly removed and my clothes would also have been taken without the intervention of a Prussian officer charged with assembling the prisoners so I lost only my shako.

At the moment of the rout, the brave Ramu was at my side and I saw him fall, his foot traversed by a ball. My memory serving me too well in this moment, I thought to act for the best by complying with his bequest and taking his shako. In this I was unfortunate, for having been unable to keep my own headdress, I was still less able to save Ramu's in the midst of the fight I have just described.

On finding the next day, that dear Ramu, who I thought was dead, was captured like me, wounded, and through my fault was without his shako and especially the contents which would have been doubly precious to him, I felt a keen regret and made my sincere apologies for my clumsiness. This excellent man took the thing at best, he told me later that he had not lost anything financially, the bills of exchange or credit entrusted to the shako having been paid later on the certificates he had provided.

Let us return to the battlefield. I lost a lot of blood, one of my sergeants, seriously wounded himself, still had the generosity to force me to take his scarf to bind my head wound, my own handkerchief wrapped my hand. This scarf was my only head-dress on the way to Königsberg.

Such was my last battle, which concluded the first day of the Battle of Leipzig.

The French Army had maintained itself in its positions, other than the one occupied by our army corps which was too weak to resist the weight of the attack directed against it. The Emperor, who loved nothing but success, was at first in a very bad temper at this failure and published a bulletin in which he did not spare our corps his criticisms, but soon the truth came to light and justice was done to us when they discovered that we had been abandoned in a contest against triple our own forces. We had, quite simply, been taken prisoner or killed at our posts and no one could ask for more of us.

Here is how Baron Fain, secretary of the cabinet of the Emperor at this time, expressed himself in the relation of that day, published in 1824, under the title of *Manuscrit de 1813*.

> The details he (Napoleon) received of the Duke of Raguse's losses are of a distressing severity. The army remained for five hours under the fire of more than one hundred pieces of cannon. The *élite* of our marine regiments perished, Generals Compans and Frederich and the Duke of Raguse himself were wounded.

And elsewhere he wrote:

> North of Leipzig, the battle was sustained no less fiercely than in the plain of the south and although the result was unfavourable the disproportion of the numbers throws here a new lustre on the French arms. We fought twenty

against sixty. The Prince of Moskowa and the Duke of Raguse did not fear to stand up, with their weak army, to the three combined armies of Blücher and the struggle lasted all day.

Our brave men held with such vigour the villages of Möckern and Grosswetteritz that the armies of Yorck and Langeron, tired of attacking, finally summoned the help of Sacken and his third army.

Our regiment was nearly destroyed in this affair, the major who commanded us and our eagle were taken. All the officers, except those who had prudently retired before the debacle, were captured or killed. The other Marine Artillery regiments suffered less, not being as we were, at the end of the attacked wing. Our flag-bearer, Mutel, who was picked up with his eagle and driven into Russia with the rest of us, often told me that, seeing the trouble, he had broken the eagle's pole and put the eagle itself under his coat to hide it if possible.

Unfortunately, when he was reached by the enemy cavalry, his artificial hump had not entirely hidden it from view and the eagle and the coat had become a trophy for our foes. Mutel, who was a fat playful boy, had escaped the battle without injury, which cast a shadow over the heroism traditionally expected of the standard bearer who would have been better off, in the opinion of several observers concerned with regimental honour, being dead or wounded, but he was not unduly upset himself for having preserved his life and limbs.

CHAPTER TWELVE

Prisoner of War

On the evening of October 16th, I arrived at night, with a number of other prisoners in the small town of Schkeuditz, situated a short distance from the Saxon frontier on the road to Halle. It was impossible to recognise anyone because of the darkness. We were huddled and horribly heaped up together, healthy, wounded and dying, in the local church where I spent the saddest night in the world, covered in blood, my thumb hanging on a shred of flesh, thirsty and hungry and in the midst of the cries and moans of other wounded.

In the morning, the wounded were taken out to be dressed in a nearby ambulance. I was one of them, and on entering this room the first person I recognised was the major, unsurprisingly in a perfectly intact condition. Masked by blood as I was, he did not recognise me at first. Be that as it may, I looked at this object of my contempt without saying a word to him and soon found more interesting acquaintances among the other officers of the regiment, many of whom were in a very sorry state. I have already said that one of this number was my compatriot, Ramu.

There were not many ways to dress my wounds, a medic, with a pair of tailors scissors, cut off what still held my thumb, put a bit of lint and light bandage on my head and hand and declared I was fit to go; a statement in accordance with my wishes; seeing so many more serious injuries I did not feel mine and the thought of staying in the midst of amputees and the dying made me shudder.

While our wounds were being dressed, the more healthy prisoners who remained in the church were subjected to a second looting by NCO's or Prussian soldiers, who, I like to believe, escaped the surveillance of their officers and who seized, without ceremony, money and clothes saved from the field of battle. It was my lucky star that delivered me from this inconvenience and I owe it to that entity to have thus preserved one *surtout* coat which was to be of the greatest use to me during the term of my captivity. In short, I was part of a large convoy of officers and soldiers, most of my arm (the infantry) which set out under the guard of a detachment of Prussian infantry, leaving in Schkeuditz my thumb (which was given, I hope, an honourable burial), several disabled comrades, including Ramu, and streets cluttered with wagons bringing the Russian and Prussian wounded from the day before, whose cries were heard in the distance.

On the 17th October 1813, we arrived at Halle, in a very bad state, starving and having eaten nothing since the morning before and exhausted by so many actions and adventures. The officers were contained on one side and the soldiers on the other in public buildings where we received some food and straw to sleep. I have never slept better than in the night of the 17th to the 18th. I felt in the morning, when I woke up, a mechanical satisfaction of not being obliged, as at the bivouac, to tug at my soldiers' coats at daybreak to make them take up their arms. My captivity and the impending anxiety of my parents, presented itself only as a second line in my mind, touched as I was by the lightness of those around me, the slightest well-being, given our survival, brought back among us gaiety and the telling of jokes.

This carelessness was an attribute of youth and military life. More seriously, I should have thought of the dangers which my country, and my family were running in this fierce war which was encompassing all of Europe. I should have especially given thanks to God who preserved for me, in the midst of so many dangers, a life from which I was so far from being worthy.

From that day we lived in an almost absolute ignorance of what was going on in the army; we did not understand German, and besides we were inclined to believe only in the success of our arms, and to treat with caution all the news which was unfavourable to the fortunes of the French Army.

Our route continued on towards Berlin. The convoy consisted of about sixty officers, a dozen of whom were of my regiment, and a few hundred soldiers from the ranks. Every day at the stopover we were incarcerated whilst on the march we were escorted by a militia detachment of *landsturm*.

My wounds, without making me very ill, made me suffer enough during the first days. I received no bandages other than those which I administered myself, helped, if needed, by some comrade. I was making lint with the clippings of cloth that I received from the compassion of my landlords. Nevertheless, I was happier than other officers, whose trousers had been taken and who made the journey from Leipzig to Berlin in under garments, since I had lost only the shako and the picturesque headdress with which I crossed all of Prussia was a headscarf all stained with blood.

In common with everyone else, in these moments of misery, I became attached to a favourite comrade with whom, through an exchange of services one alleviates misfortune and distracts oneself. Mine was a captain of my regiment by the name of Thouvenin. He was about my age, he had an amiable character and I remained in his debt, not by the use of his purse, for we had neither the penny nor the other, but by the kindness with which he took care of what my arm in a sling prevented me doing for myself.

We had therefore passed together, in spite of fate, more than one pleasant moment, our sufferings even lent us a laugh; it was thus that one day my friend, Thouvenin, feeling ill, did not eat; I said to him very earnestly and with a penetrating tone,

'How happy you are Thouvenin! You're not hungry, that I would like to be sick like you!'

This exclamation, which a malnourished stomach took from me in good faith, has more than once amused us in times of plenty and Thouvenin did not fail to remind me of it. This friend is now second in command of a regiment of Marine Artillery. Since my return to civil life, I had for a while kept up a correspondence with him, but it has now ceased. I know not by the fault of which of us two that has come to pass, but I sincerely regret it.

It was from between two ranks of *landsturm* that we saw Berlin, to be shut up in a barracks where we had communication only with Jews who, for some *groschen*, (10 *pfennig* pieces), came to buy the cast-offs of the prisoners, who were happy to be able to obtain a little more bread made possible by these transactions.

Madame Trembley de Ribaupierre, whom I call my saviour because, intimate friend of my parents, she took care of me with the most touching activity in my misfortune. Having long resided in Berlin where her husband was a distinguished academic, she had made good friends both among Prussian high society and with French emigrants. She took advantage of these connections on my behalf, both at that time and later on.

It was through research that she had undertaken through her friends in Prussia that my parents, without news and in mortal anxiety since the Battle of Leipzig, learned that I had crossed Berlin as a prisoner of war. If it had been in time, the order to stop at the passage of the Prussian capital and to make me stay there until peace would have been made; but as I said, her research only resulted in showing my passing and she could not discover where I was or where I was going. However, Madame Trembley's obliging activity was not quite wasted for she benefited Ramu, who, recovered from his wound, was detained in Berlin and lived there pleasantly, being introduced into those families to which I would have been recommended.

We only stayed a day or two in Berlin and our convoy was directed to the north of Prussia. As we moved away from the theatre of war, the precautions to contain us became superfluous and we ended up billeted in the homes of private individuals who were required to feed us. Some militia cavalry were our escort. The Prussians were then animated by a violent hatred of the French. They were ruined by the war, so that the *burgh-*

ers charged with feeding us paid as little as possible for it; their poverty or bad faith literally starved us. How many times did I not see myself sent to a landlord in a bad mood to ask modestly 'a little more bread?' which was ordinarily refused me.

This crossing of Prussia was arduous because of the irritation of the people, who, not content to starve us often also insulted us. For example, in a small town, I believe it was Schweinfurt, we were placed in a queue in the town square to receive our lodgings when a large gentleman of the upper class came by with some friends to lavish us with insults and spit in our faces. It was impossible for us to resist this abuse in the middle of a rising population that only wanted an excuse to cause us harm.

Our major, for his part, was kicked in the backside when he turned his back on this scene, a humiliation which contrasted with his past arrogance. My turn would probably have come without the intervention of our guards who put an end to this disorder. I will conclude my comments about the major by saying that he obtained, because of his rank I suppose, the authorisation to leave us to remain in Prussia, but he crowned his relations with us by a trait well worthy of him.

On the 16th October, when, crowded into the church of Schkeuditz, we still feared the looting, a lieutenant of the regiment thought to put his small change safe in his boot, while begging the major to keep some *napoleons* for him. The poor man was only changing the identity of the Cossack! The major never did give him his gold and he left our convoy without saying a word to him, abandoning him to all privations.

It was at the end of November that we entered Königsberg. Until then, poorly received by the Prussians, I experienced in this city a first act of kindness on their part. My pretty dilapidated costume and especially my strange headdress attracted the attention of an honest *bourgeois* who pressed me to accept a green leather cap, which he made in a shop. I would have absolutely refused this gift if I could explain myself in German, however this difficulty of communication and the fear of offending this good man with a refusal prevented me from doing so. I took the cap from him with an exaggerated display of gratitude.

Unfortunately, I found that this cap was irritating the wound on my forehead which was, it is true, closed but still sensitive. The idea came to me to use this gift more practically by cutting it and sewing the pieces as best I could to close a certain 'window' in my trousers where the November cold caused an indescribable discomfort in an inexpressible place. It was going from one extreme to the other! Ah! If my generous benefactor had come to ascertain with his own eyes the use of his gift, what would not have been my embarrassment to show him the sweet spectacle!

We learned in Memmel from the Military Governor's mouth that we were going to Russia. This was the subject of very sad reflections; the habit of dying of hunger would join that of dying of cold in the country where winter had devoured a French Army.

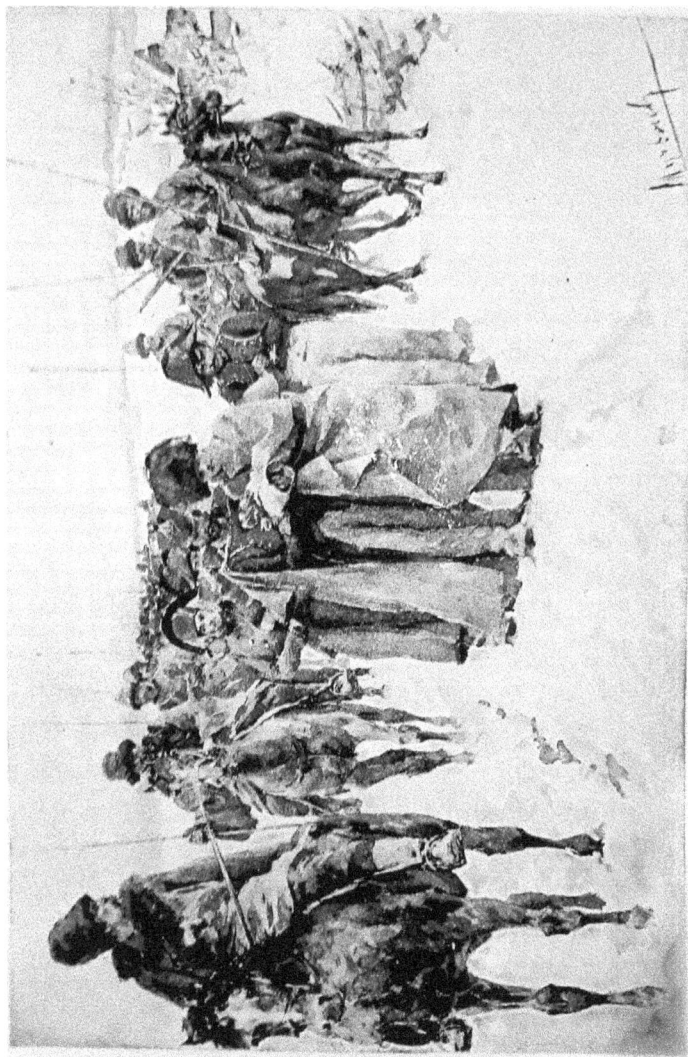

MARCHING PRISONERS

CHAPTER THIRTEEN

Captive into Russia

The snow began for us in Pollangen, precisely on the Russian border. This ominous appearance dispelled, for the moment, the little gaiety which remained to us.

Our black forecasts however, were exaggerated for the beneficent genius of the Emperor Alexander tempered Russia for us. According to his generous orders each prisoner received a sufficient allowance to obtain warm clothes when he entered Russia and also received a daily allowance for his food. The reward was, for the convoy of which I was a part, sixty *francs* per officer without distinction of rank and the daily pay of about five *sous* from France.

With these sixty *francs* I could buy myself a coarse woollen *pelisse*, a quilted cap with ear flaps, fur lined shoes, gloves with fur inside and out and finally two shirts and a pair of woollen socks. I even had some money left over. The change of linen was a great pleasure because it gave me the opportunity to rid myself of the vermin that had cruelly tormented me when, wounded, I could neither undress nor scratch myself.

On 28th December, 1813, we arrived at Riga. The winter was then very severe and the River Duna served as a great frozen road. I had the opportunity in this city to visit a Livonian noble, named Baron Mengden, to whom I was introduced by Thouvenin who had made himself, I do not know how, recommended to him. Having learned that the baron had his mother staying in Lausanne, the purpose of my visit was to ask him to

A REGIMENT OF COSSACKS ON THE MARCH

send a letter, addressed for simplicity, to my Aunt Rieu in Rolle. This was the first opportunity I had to write to my parents since my capture.

My letter, dated December 30, 1813, arrived at its destination only on May 3rd, 1814, either by the negligence of the baron or also the difficulty of communications in time of war. However late it was, it gave the first details of my fate to my parents, who had only vaguely learned that I was a prisoner of war.

When I left Riga on January 1, 1814, I was sorry to leave Thouvenin, who availed himself of Baron Mengden's offer of asylum which several other officers also elected to accept. But that apparent good fortune did not long benefit them, for sent to the lands of the baron, they suffered so much from the bitter cold and boredom that after a few days they asked to resume their journey. Nevertheless, I was definitively thereafter separated from Thouvenin, who was then part of another convoy.

From Riga, we formed a convoy comprised only of officers, having a Russian officer and three Bashkirs to conduct us. These Cossacks were a novelty for us; their headdress consisted of a high cylindrical cap of green cloth, jacket of the same, Asiatic style trousers. Their weapons were a sword, a quiver and a bow. They were good people for whom we only had praise ourselves, their main occupation being to provide us with sleds or wagons, to distribute our lodgings *en route* and to protect us, if need be, against the insults of the people which fortunately was rarely necessary.

From Riga, we were directed to Witebsk, a city in Russian Poland. Napoleon had stayed there in 1812, and had there the first serious battle after the entry of the French Army into Russia. The journey from Riga to Witebsk was the most painful part of our journey because of the cold weather. Travelling a path covered with frozen snow, on peasant sleds, uncovered and furnished with bales of hay, there was no way to walk, because of the ice. Nor was it possible to extend ones numbed limbs. The temperature, which went down to 27 or 30 degrees *Réaumer*, became intolerable, especially when the wind blew severely.

It was then necessary to cover one's nose and ears as best as one could to prevent them from freezing, and as for the feet which were the focus of the main suffering, one sought to stretch them as much as possible by waving them about and hiding them under the sled hay. I was not without fear for mine, although I had stuffed shoes over the boots. The vapour of the breath was changed into ice cubes which clung to the hair, to the beard, to everything around the face and then we looked exactly like those winter figures we see on the covers of almanacs.

As soon as we came upon an inhabited house, we stopped to stock up on heat, and woe to him who, having a numb limb, approached the stove too quickly for he was soon experiencing severe pain. I even saw one of our comrades, whose ears were beginning to freeze and who wanted to heat them, suddenly covered with swellings in this part, absolutely similar to those of burns. These swellings subsequently burst, so he had living flesh in the ears and a wound which was slow to heal. More than one nose and more than one half frozen foot were successfully treated by rubbing them with snow. I did not have any accidents like that because I was well 'caulked' with my pelisse, my ear muffs and my stuffed shoes, also I was careful to keep my face well covered up to the eyes with the help of my clothes.

The days being very short, we did not easily make great strides, so that we reached Witebsk only in the course of February 1814, to stay there about six weeks. Our daily allowance enabled us to buy, either at the market or from our landlords, the foodstuffs that we then prepared ourselves for our meal. We met, as a result, by squads to make a better and more economical kitchen, each one taking turns for the duty of cook. For my part, I made more than one excellent broth, including lean soups, of which our *bourgeois* kitchens would have had to blush, supposing that they were susceptible to a colour other than that of water, and I still see myself haggling in bad Russian for eggs or potatoes in the public square.

It goes without saying that there was no question of wine or other spirit to drink, it was substituted by the less heady beverage of Russian households, named *quasse*, a kind of water acidulated by the fermentation of a little barley flour mixed in it and which doesn't have a disagreeable taste.

I did a little study at Witebsk of the Polish Jews who populated the city. I was lodged with an individual of this class, together with another comrade. The accommodation of our host consisted of two rooms. In one, he slept with his wife and four or five children; the other served as a kitchen, living room, refectory, study room etc; we slept on the floor covered with a felt saddle having our clothes for a mattress, sheets and blankets, the first object came for a pillow. An old *Rabbi*, who came during the day to teach the children to read, was careful to peel his vermin, during the lesson, on to the floor where we spent the night. Comfort is relative and we became used to everything, including the dirt. We did not have the idea to be unhappy after an icy journey when we had a share in the heat of the oven of our Jew. He and his family looked at us with the most indifferent eyes, and did not go away except at the sight of our coins which paid for the items they provided us.

The steam baths were here in profusion, as in all Russia. I used them with pleasure in the public baths, which cannot be more economical, I think even free; they served our purpose of personal cleanliness and that of our clothes which we exposed to a degree of heat sufficient to kill the vermin, for they were our great plague as I have said. Steam is produced in these baths by water that is sprayed on red hot stones in the oven and there is a degree of heat, more or less strong, by placing them more or less high on the benches arranged for this purpose. When the body is dripping with sweat and the blood is well heated, it is sprayed with ice water delights, which does no harm if one takes care to then resume one's place by the heat of the oven.

Witebsk offered us no other distraction than rest, the frozen countryside about it offered few attractions whilst the city is a hovel populated by greedy and dirty Jews. These Jews have a commendable emulation to deceive in the markets, of which they are the inevitable agents, all those who are not their co-religionists.

I talked about a fellow house-mate and I must add that I did not change any of them during the rest of my captivity in Russia. He was a lieutenant of my regiment, named Gerfau, a young man of a good nature and endowed with a lively and original imagination which amused me greatly. We have made together, besides that of Russia, more than one trip to the 'land of the chimeras' (Jean-Jacques Rousseau–a retreat of private imagination), personifying, attributing language to everyone in the world and laughing like madmen, to the astonishment of those who, still very innocent, did not have the key to our jokes.

At the end of March, 1814, we finally left Witebsk, heading for Smolensk, a city in ancient Russia formerly known for its thick walls. It was famous in the campaign of 1812 because of the battle fought under those walls and bore the recent traces of the ravages of war and the fire which had burned two thirds of the city. Nothing is easier than the burning of a city in Russia, although the houses are generally separated by fields of crops, and raised, at most, a floor in small towns. These houses are built of wood; beams trimmed with an axe and superimposed horizontally to form the walls, the moss fills the interstices; the whole is usually made of wood or thatch so nothing is more combustible than this ensemble. The strong winds which prevail in these lowlands often make rescue impossible and promote the spread of fire.

Winter was not over, but it was mild enough to be very tolerable, so that, lodged as usual with peasants and with the single 'oven' which shapes the home of a whole family, we had almost to complain of the intensity of the heat. The arrangements of the inhabitants in the 'oven' is of the greatest simplicity; the whole family sleeps about a vast stove without a chimney; when the stove is heated, the smoke comes out where it can, and to breathe freely one must lie down on the floor, the smoke preferring to occupy the upper region. Fixed benches were arrayed along the walls; these benches, on which we stretched our *pelisses*, served us as beds. In a corner is always the image of St Nicholas and that of the Virgin, whom everyone salutes upon entering by the sign of the cross, accompanied by a bend from the waist. We are not slow to learn that, lying on the benches, one should never turn one's feet towards the pictures. This pose, regarded as disrespectful, would have been viewed badly by the natives.

On a day in Smolensk, one of the Lords of the place, named Schiroff, having the rank of Major, invited all the prisoner convoy to spend the night in his *château*, where he gave us supper and plenty of straw in a vast room where we slept. He had a pretty and excellent wife. He told me first of the liberation of Geneva by the Austrians, but the news gave me no pleasure. The idea of seeing my homeland returned to freedom did not come to my mind, as I had fully identified myself with the objectives of the French by this time.

Besides its ruined state, the earlier passage of the French Army was still visible in Smolensk by the presence of a huge fleet of wagons, caissons, fourgons and carriages abandoned in the retreat and which now covered a large square. It seemed as though one wandered into the next world, reading on these carriages the names of the generals, army corps etc to whom they had once belonged.

We could have expected to find much annoyance against the French on a road followed, in 1812, by the army of that nation, but we had very rarely had cause to complain, rather, it was beyond Moscow where the French Army had never reached that we found a bad disposition against us. For the most part this abuse was in general reduced to a few verbal insults, to which we would respond with abundance and exhausting the worst Russian vocabulary when we were regaled with 'French dogs,' 'Paris is taken' etc. At the same time, it must be admitted that some of our comrades behaved with French self-conceit and thoughtlessness often striking the peasants for the slightest reason which, in more than one other country, would have led to serious reprisals for them.

Our route to Moscow passed through the towns of Dorogobus, Wiasma and Mojaisk. It was on the outskirts of this last town that we saw the traces of the famous battle fought in 1812, (Borodino), the place was still indicated by half destroyed redoubts and some debris of weapons. We had with us for a guide an infantry captain who had the unfortunate singular destiny to pass safe and sound through the campaign and retreat of 1812 only to come and be captured at Leipzig and to begin again all the steps he had previously trodden of this distant land.

We arrived at the gates of Moscow on May 1, 1814. That day, without the evidence of a spring transition, summer began with its heat and we were present at the breakup of the ice on the River Moscowa. We did not enter Moscow itself, but we were made to stay for a fortnight in a neighbouring village, from where we could see the innumerable cupolas of the partly burned city, burning ourselves likewise with the desire to see it more closely.

This desire was superficially satisfied, for at first, we traversed Moscow, mounted on wagons and duly escorted since we were not without fear as to the disposition of the population towards us. Nothing happened, however, with only a few insults and we were able to convince ourselves, while crossing the Kremlin, that this famous citadel, which the French bulletins had 'blown up', was still quite healthily standing. Despite the rapidity of our passage I will never forget the impression made on me by these streets of Moscow, lined with charred ruins, in the middle of which, like oases, rose some beautiful buildings, rebuilt to a high standard or saved from the fire which destroyed so many others. They were still populated with the shadows of that beautiful French Army which the cold had petrified so recently. In the distance neighbourhoods remained intact, bearing the character of all Russian cities, that is to say, intermixed with cultivated land.

With Moscow behind us what was the purpose or end of our trip? That we did not know, and that was what worried us because the passers-by told us that we were going to be sent to Siberia. The opinion, it is true, was not official but hearsay, but it froze us in imagination.

Beyond Moscow the heat became stifling. The roads were covered with a black dust which the wagons or the wind set in motion and which fixed itself, as a mask, upon the face. Mask for mask by comparison, it was better than that of icicles and the verdure of the fields had an incontestable advantage over the sad monotony of vast plains covered with snow. Our sleds had been converted into little carriages with wooden axles, ungreased and screaming in a disorderly manner as we progressed.

Here, more traces of war, more ruins and debris, the commodities were cheap and plentiful, so that our five *sous* sufficed for our food and the maintenance of our shoes.

I do not pretend to describe Russia. Our old continent is so well known, and my means of seeing and judging things were so limited that I would be reduced to common places or inaccuracies. Unlike preachers, who must refrain from putting themselves in their sermons I make it a point to speak much more about myself than anything else.

After going through Wladimir, the only city of any appearance on our way, we arrived, in the middle of June, 1814, at Simbirsk, a town situated on the Volga, about 160 leagues east of Moscow, and capital of the government of the same name.

We found there several French prisoners who dated from the retreat of 1812. It was a sign that we would go no further. We were provisionally billeted in private homes, but soon we were assigned to barracks in an uninhabited house, which had belonged, it was said, to some noble exiled in Siberia. I was, at the time lodged with two comrades at the house of a rich merchant of the place, named Twerdichef.

This good man, interested in us, obtained permission from the governor to keep us at his home. I do not really know which of our merits captivated him, unless it was our good looks, for he did not speak French, we did not speak Russian and could only make signs to him. Not having asked for this act of benevolence, he pleasantly surprised us all the more. We had the use of a room, furnished with the inevitable straw as a bed, and a place at the kitchen fire to cook the food we bought.

Our host invited us to his table once, and generally had with us a benevolent relationship for which we were touched and thankful, and yet we had the mortification of refusing him a request that he made to us, to make a firework for the feast of the Emperor Alexander whose date was coming up soon. It was clear he was relying on our experience as artillery officers. But he counted without his guests, we knew just enough between us to make a firecracker, but nothing more. Instead of simply agreeing, which would have been more honest, we had the false pride of making an excuse, entrenching ourselves behind a pretended national pride which did not allow us to contribute at the party of a sovereign who was an enemy of France. I do not know what the dear man thought of our far-fetched motive, but he at least had the politeness to be content with it.

Simbersk did not deviate from the layout of the other cities of Russia; a mixture of houses of both beautiful and pitiful appearance, separated by spaces under cultivation, and iron churches with green cupolas. No location on the River Volga dominates the opposite bank which reveals the expanse of vast plains without habitations. We almost feel in the vicinity of the *steppes* of Asia. The Volga itself is a broad and majestic river, whose almost imperceptible current is favourable to the numerous boats that go up and down during the summer. Its waters, in which I once tried to bathe, seemed to be very cold, even during a very hot summer, and I preferred the water of a little river which flows near the town.

During our stop in Simbersk, I learned one day through the chief of police, that it was requested in a Russian paper that my presence be reported. I have since learned that it was the result of a step taken by my saviour, Madame Trembley, who had employed for that the good offices of a brother, established in Russia, and honoured in the diplomacy of this Empire, M. de Ribaupierre.

However, I did not take advantage of the notice. Peace was made by then and our return to France was soon certain. Besides I wanted to stay with my comrades in misfortune. An officer, who was leaving for France, had at last taken up a letter for my parents, and I knew that their anxiety would be just as quickly calmed in this way, as indeed it was.

CHAPTER FOURTEEN

Peace and the Return

After a month's stay in Simbersk, and the European war being over, the happy moment of our departure for France arrived, which took place towards the middle of July 1814. We had for an escort, the same officer and the same Bashkirs, and our convoy had increased by several officers, prisoners from the retreat of 1812, and some soldiers who had attached themselves to the service of the officers to travel more conveniently.

I learned that among these 'recruits' there was an officer who called himself a Genevese and I immediately went to rub shoulders with my fellow countryman. I met a small young man who told me he was to be called Montfort, and who could never answer my questions about his family and about Geneva in a very satisfactory manner. I did not further deepen this mystery, having learned that this alleged officer was, at most, a sub-officer and besides, finding in him only a very reserved chatter, I let him go completely. I do not know if he found himself surprised to find a compatriot on whom he had perhaps not counted on.

Our return did not take place by the same road as the arrival for we were directed further south *via* the Duchy of Warsaw. After passing through Tula, Mohilev and Minsk we arrived at Bialystock, a town in Polish Russia, frontier of the Duchy. With the exception of Tula, where there are quite a few large artillery foundries, we did not see anything remarkable on this journey through a country that was uniformly flat and often forested with forlorn fir trees.

From Simbersk to Bialystock there are about 380 leagues, which we travelled in fifty days; this lasted until the beginning of September 1814.

Our way of travelling had not changed, always on peasant carts, lodged in the villages and spending our nights more willingly on the hay of the barn than the bench of the room.

My comrade, Gerfau, and I had added a reinforcement to our travelling life, attaching to ourselves a Russian speaking Neapolitan soldier who had an *ex-cantiniere* wife. We were thus free from the worry of seeking our lodging, which the husband went to reconnoitre in advance, and from that of preparing our meals, which the woman was doing better than we could.

The Party spirit, which was dividing France, was already visible among the officers of the convoy. Those who honestly admitted the new politics and believed in the restoration of the Bourbons and the fall of Napoleon were reputed 'Royalists', while those who did not quarrel with the vaunted invincibility of Napoleon and refused to believe in his decline were called 'Bonapartists'. I think that if the trip had been prolonged it would have eventually come to blows between these two groups.

Bialystock, on our arrival, was encumbered with prisoners of war who were concentrated there in order to issue them successively road maps for France. We were not the first to arrive and had to wait for our turn for twenty days, crammed into private homes which had been changed into barracks. Add to this that the congestion was increased by the passage of the Russian Army returning from France. The return of this army, very beautiful and perfectly maintained, disturbed the hopes of our stubborn 'Bonapartists' more than a little.

Finally, at the beginning of October 1814, I found myself duly placed with some comrades of my choice, given a road map and we set out joyously and without escort, as light as birds let out of their cages. I hastened to forget the little Russian I had learned to shop for food and to answer insults, I did not have too much German to forget, but moreover I heard this language again with pleasure as it seemed to bring me closer to my own country.

In the Duchy of Warsaw, it was the language of the Jews with which we alone had to deal, as they accumulate all kinds of commerce. These Jews, dirtier than anywhere else, were usually our landlords and the precautions to be taken to avoid scabies and the vermin were without number. I have seen nothing like their pharisaic tricks to evade their religious law; for example, being unable to trade on the Sabbath, the merchants received the money for what they sold on that day on a dish or on the hand covered with an apron.

As for the Polish peasants, we vainly sought in them the pride of the soldiers of their country. Their bearing was extremely servile and their misery deep. I found myself, a very shabby prisoner, having my feet kissed by one of them to whom I was giving a piece of bread. Their homes were Noah's arks, where they live together with chickens, calves and pigs, and I never managed to swallow a piece of their bread, composed of leaves and earth where the flour makes up the lesser part. When we compare this with the clean and clear air of the Russian peasant, we understand that the much-regretted freedom of the Poles has only benefited the nobles. The military state, compared to this life of abjection, is a life of enjoyment, and these same men, finding themselves happy, become excellent soldiers.

We saw at Warsaw the Grand Duke Constantine, Governor of the Duchy. This prince sometimes had benevolent views, but spoiled that in abrupt or bizarre ways. We stayed one day in Warsaw, then filled with Russian troops, and we left for Kalisch, a city on the border of the Duchy with Prussia.

Soon we reached the theatre of our exploits in 1813, crossing Silesia and Saxony, seeing again Bunzlau, Gnadenberg, Bautzen, Dresden, places that witnessed our combats, today witnesses of our misery, I could also say of our joy, because the idea of seeing our homes again consoled us for everything we had endured.

On entering Dresden, Prince Repnin, who was then Governor of Saxony on behalf of the Allied powers, found himself on our way. I do not know if it was by design or by chance, though the latter is most likely. He stopped us to ask a few questions about our situation and destination.

This prince, a favourite of the Emperor Alexander, and then at the height of his honours, scarcely anticipated that twenty-six years later he would come to recommend himself to the benevolence of one of those prisoners, upon whom he scarcely cast a pitying glance. Who could have imagined that one day I would see him, disgraced and exiled, come to visit me as the first Trustee of the Republic of Geneva?

CHAPTER FIFTEEN

My Arrival in France

Our road map directed us to Mayence; but this city being encumbered with troops, we were made to make a detour by Mannheim, where we re-passed the Rhine to reach Strasbourg *via* Landau. We laid foot on the soil of France on November 2, 1814, after a year and eighteen days in captivity.

The journey from Simbersk to Strasbourg lasted three and a half months, including the stops, and the distance covered was about six hundred and fifty leagues. The journey from Leipzig to Simbersk, passing through Riga, had lasted eight months, including all the stops and especially that of more than six weeks at Witebsk, and we had travelled about six hundred and twenty leagues.

It is evident that we had been much slower going than on the way back, either because of the shortness of the winter days and the rigour of the cold, or because, more free when we came back, we were eager to see the homeland again and travelled at up to three times the pace.

In short, our journey, since the Battle of Leipzig, had been about twelve hundred and seventy leagues without it costing us a penny. We were, it is true, burdened neither with money nor with baggage, the Cossacks having had the kindness to shelter us from thieves.

Our incredulous 'Bonapartists' were at last convinced of the arrival of a new order when they saw the French troops wearing white cockades and the *Fleur de Lys* in the button holes of all the officers. What changes there had been in our absence! Our astonishment was equal to that of fairy-tale sleepers who awake from a spell after a few hundred years! France was now reduced to the cramped limits of the old kingdom, which after all our successes seemed most paltry. On the throne sat a Bourbon whose existence we had scarcely suspected, and the great Napoleon, passing from the sublime to the ridiculous, was now king of only a little island in the Mediterranean after having ruled over most of Europe. Finally, our own personal destinies were called into question by the dismissal of part of the army in which we belonged.

Foreigners, we discovered, were being dismissed from the French services which meant I found myself without a place after so many seemingly pointless endeavours. So, it was with a heart split between this sad reflection and the pleasure of rejoining my family that I took leave of my companions in misfortune when each of us finally took the road to his own home.

As for me, I set off on foot, with a map and without money, for Paris, where I had to collect eagerly awaited letters from Geneva, together with pecuniary resources, which were more prosaic than news but nonetheless indispensable. At last, I had the inexpressible joy of finding a large envelope containing that letter at my address. With what delight I devoured it

I learned that everything was going well at home, Geneva revelled in its freedom and my parents were in perfect health. What exceeded my expectations was that I was to keep my place in the service of France. My saviour, Mme Trembley, had persuaded one of her closest friends, whom she had known in Berlin as an *émigré* and was now in great favour because of the restoration, to take active and fruitful steps on my behalf. Accordingly, my parents had obtained official assurance that I would be retained in the Marine Artillery. The friend I am referring to was the Duc d'Escars.

It is quite true that I was only half employed, having to spend six months with the regiment on full pay and six months on half pay. The peculiarity of this arrangement, which was not confined to me, was softened by the prospect of before long gaining full employment with successive vacancies in officer places. In any case, it was a particular favour for me for the excellence of the Swiss brought to the service had in the main been excluded from the French Army.

I metamorphosed, in Paris, from the chrysalis I had become into a veritable butterfly as soon as I had some money to spend and introduced myself to the Duc de Noailles, an old acquaintance of my family, for whom I had a letter of recommendation.

I also paid a visit to M. Chabanon, First Secretary of the Navy Department, who facilitated the settlement of my outstanding pay arrears. To find myself at the head of a few crowns after being in destitution for more than a year was almost to be a millionaire!

The Duc de Noailles persuaded me dine with his daughter, the Countess of Montagu, who also knew my family, and the lioness of the moment, Sister Martha, sister of charity, who had been satiated with presents, and even decorations by the allied sovereigns for having devoted herself with remarkable zeal to the care of the wounded of all nations during the campaign of 1814. She was a good woman, not associating her mind to her kindness, and one for whom the modesty of a hospitable woman was a finer adornment than the decorations she received or her place at the tables of the great.

After dessert the duke took me to his study with a solemnity that made my heart beat faster, then, signing a certificate of the *l'Ordre du Lys*, (The Order of the Lily), of which he had a stack in white, he put it in my name and gave it to me by hanging the silver lily on the white ribbon. The good duke thought to fill me with joy, while suppressing a grimace I gave him a polite thanks. It is proper to say that this order was only a cockade that was given to whoever wanted it and that the officers of the former Imperial Army regarded it more as a forced humiliation than as a mark of honour.

CHAPTER SIXTEEN

Home To Geneva

I climbed into the coach bound for Geneva at the end of November 1814, with few worries on my mind and with a lighter purse. I arrived, as it transpired, earlier than I had announced or was expected.

Profiting from this circumstance when I arrived at my home, I announced myself to the good Henrietta, who opened the door without recognising me, as someone who had to speak with M. Rieu. I was determined to play the role of a stranger for a while with my father, to better enjoy his surprise if he did not unmask me at first sight, but as the door of his room opened I could not, and forgetting my projected role I took the more natural one of a son who sees his father again after so many events and worries.

My voice had hardly been heard, rather, than as if by a single spring, the doors of all the other rooms opened at once and I felt myself almost smothered in the arms of my father, my mother, my brother Charles and my sister Elisa. It was a unique moment in my life!

A few days spent in the paternal home quickly restored me to all my old habits. I was the Jean Louis of old and I am surprised myself when I think about it, remembering how little, thanks to the reserve of my character, I had absorbed from contact abroad during six consecutive years of absence.

The years had scarcely marked my parents. They had, on the other hand, changed my brother and sister remarkably. It was the same with the interior of the Republic of Geneva now restored to liberty. Everything was then zeal and concord. Everyone wanted to have his share of public affairs, each put on an importance for themselves which was sometimes exaggerated. It was a nascent kingdom of commissions, committees of all kinds for a silence of fifteen years had loosed all languages and preserved their freshness. It was to whom would deliberate, discuss, vote etc. The sentence was made with unmixed pleasure, I do not say for the listeners, who found the time spent listening to be lost.

I drove one day in the carriage to Nyon with two respectable citizens, who, during the whole trip were talking about a very important deliberation, with which their circle seemed very pre-occupied. I thought that I, a novice, would have to deal with, at least, two trustees. I then discovered that they were two members of the Chamber of Cleanliness, then charged only to record the night-spoil pots which had been unduly thrown out of windows.

The Councillors of State gave up neither the tri-corns nor the swords of their offices. I even believe that they kept them on when they were going to bed, and the Trustee of the Guard, identifying himself with the letter of his title, passed every day, at noon, a review of the guard mounting which a council-major in epaulettes was parading. We were living in a hive of bees, minus the queen.

I was still very French in my ways and thinking, very unenthusiastic about this republican display, which sometimes bored me thoroughly, and my poor father who was himself a very good republican, but spoke little and dreading long deliberations, sometimes agreed with me.

Alas! When, having become a good Genevan I later reflected on these moments of patriotism without partisanship, even with their accompaniment of small ridiculous little things, how much I regretted this happy time when the people of Geneva, purified by the ordeal of misfortune, had no other passion than that of the Country and a wise freedom! The impure breath of the press and radicalism had not yet passed through it to corrupt, by wanton discontent, calumny and hatred, public as well as individual happiness.

I found in Geneva two comrades from the Polytechnic School who were still undecided about their future. One was Dufour, captain in the engineers, now Quartermaster-General of the Confederation; the other, Audeoud, captain of artillery, died in 1840 as a captain of the paid Guard. I also found my countryman, Captain Ramu, who had, as I said, spent the time of his captivity in Berlin. This good man, who had arrived in Geneva a long time before me, had been, as one may imagine, thoroughly questioned by my parents, who had liked him because of his modesty and his simple and unpretentious language. A premier education, which had not been pushed too far, even gave to his words a *naïve* and sometimes amusing turn. That's how he had always stimulated others to smile, when asked him if I looked like my sister Elisa, he replied that, 'I gave him a little air from the bottom'.

When he presented himself as a candidate for an officer's place as a paid guard in the garrison, we were very happy to openly support him. He died of a chest disease a few years later, still being a paid captain.

CHAPTER SEVENTEEN

The Return of the Emperor

After a winter spent in Geneva at balls and Sunday societies, I was at Rolle, at my aunt's, where I enjoyed at the same time the society of Madame Trembley, my saviour, and her daughters, when unexpectedly the news came of the landing of Napoleon at Cannes and the pronounced movement in France that was in his favour.

My own position at once became quite embarrassing. My memories were with Napoleon and I was not very fervent in my support for the Bourbons. On the other hand, all those that surrounded me in Geneva and Rolle, starting with my parents, were wound up in the highest degree against the 'Usurper' as he was then called, and it must be admitted that the Genevans had some reason to tremble for the continuance their embryonic freedom given his ultimate success.

As a French soldier I could not remain neutral, I had to take sides. In the end, I took that of the supposedly legitimate monarchy and decided to leave for Paris in the beginning of March 1815. I took a *post-chaise* together with Louis Rillet, since Rilliet-Constant and Cadet De Vincy, today Vincy-Alliez. The first was then in the bodyguard of Louis XVIII, the second was an officer of Cent-Suisses, of the King's Guard.

Burdened down with worries as we were in the beginning, we cheered ourselves prodigiously on the way through the countryside. It was impossible to be sad in the company of Rilliet for the *naïve*, good natured de Vincy did not spoil anything.

I remember that on one occasion the *post-chaise* was bogged down in the middle of a side road so that it became necessary to get off and lend a hand to the postilion to help remove it from the cloying rut. Rilliet and I got on one wheel and placed de Vincy on the other, Rilliet and I agreeing that we would only make mock efforts of exertion while we encouraged the ardour of our comrade's efforts, who was saying as he strained 'Good game, good money.' After we had made him continue this as a physical exercise for some time to our great entertainment, quite unsuccessfully needless to say, we had pity on his efforts and employed some peasants from the neighbourhood to liberate us.

We also amused ourselves greatly with an encounter we had, to our great surprise, near Nantua, with two brave gentlemen, The Chevalier du Puech and M. Soret-Goudet, both officers of the old regime, married for a long time and established in Geneva. These two champions had left Geneva two or three days before us to offer their arms to the throne and the altar, as they were then called. Unfortunately, they had arrived in Lyon at the same time as Napoleon and, despairing of the holy cause, had not thought it necessary to go further. So, they turned back with all the signs of greater disappointment, to reassure their women folk.

This very appropriate distress and appetite with which they hurried an excellent supper with us in Nantua made us laugh for a long time. We were not the only ones, for it was said in Geneva that Puech, making the history of this abortive expedition, said he had gone up with Soret on a barrel to see the entry of Napoleon into Lyons and that Soret, interrupting him, exclaimed indignantly, 'forgive me, my friend, it was good on a coach.'

As for us, who had the advantage of being younger and not married, we could not turn back like them, and as Lyons was closed to us, we decided to cross the road from Dijon to Paris by the crossroads *via* Lons-le-Saunier.

The road was not good, and it was not without loss of time that we reached Lons-le-Saunier, precisely at the moment when a corps, of which Marshal Ney was to take command, was assembled to bar the passage to Napoleon. It was immediately evident that this force would serve as an escort and not as an obstacle to the ex-Emperor. Everywhere the soldiers exclaimed Bonapartist cries and insults for the Bourbons.

When our post-chaise left Lons-le-Saunier after having obtained a relay with great difficulty, Marshal Ney arrived there and the drum recalled the troops he was to review. We now know that the marshal, after having promised Louis XVIII in Paris to bring Napoleon back in an iron cage, unexpectedly pronounced himself for Napoleon in this review and in so doing dictated his own death sentence which was carried out on the return of the Bourbons after the defeat at Waterloo. However glorious the military career of this marshal had once been, this act on his part was, none the less, an unjustifiable treason.

Ney would probably never have been able to persuade his army corps to fight Napoleon, but after the promise he had made to the king, his imperative duty was to withdraw his person, if he could not execute it. The death sentence pronounced against him was therefore just and inevitable, but Louis XVIII, more wisely advised, ought to have commuted this irreparable punishment, for the sake of a name which so much glory surrounded and which was so dear to his soldiers.

In Dijon, during our passage, half of the inhabitants were in the white cockade and the other half in the tricolour cockade. The frightened city prefect, anxious not to be caught between them, had his post-chaise hitched up ready to flee. In a word, nothing was more precarious than the state of mind in this city. The direct route to Paris became, because of the foment among the population, excessively risky and it was necessary, for the sake of prudence, to change our route and to travel *via* Langres.

Napoleon's influence did not extend as far as this city. It was still weak, at least. Everyone on the new road was still cautious. Throwing our training as officers aside we decided upon some selfish amusement. At each of our relays we were surrounded by a crowd of local 'politicians' anxiously asking for news of Napoleon's march. The poor people did not know that in us they were dealing with ruthless pranksters who were cold-bloodedly ready to tell the most absurd lies which were diametrically contrary to reality. All this intelligence was welcomed open mouthed, and we would go back in our chaise and laugh until we arrived at the next relay.

We arrived in Paris on March 18, 1815, and after having settled in the same hotel everyone departed to settle his own business. I went, for my part, to the Ministry of the Navy, where I found a register, open for a sort of special battalion, which was to train those navy officers present in Paris. Having registered, I found myself in a company which was to be commanded by Commander Counard, an old acquaintance under whose command I had been in the battalion organised on the Isle de Ré. It was not without pleasure that I also found my excellent comrade in misfortune, Thouvenin.

Paris, at that time, apparently, offered the spectacle of the greatest enthusiasm for the Royal cause, indeed, a man had been stunned by a blow with an umbrella in front of the Tuilleries for inopportunely shouting out '*Vive Napoléon!*' At the *Théâtre Français* where I was, the actors sang the song in the mode of '*Vive Henri IV*' which the stalls spontaneously repeated while the ladies in the boxes waved their white handkerchiefs.

On the 19th of March, 1815, the improvised battalion of which I was a member, met in the morning, and was conducted to the Place du Carrousel, in front of the central balcony of the Tuilleries Palace. Louis XVIII soon appeared on the balcony, walking with great difficulty because of his swollen legs. He saluted us affectionately, but with a very sad air about him, and withdrew in the midst of cries of '*Vive le Roi*' issuing from the bosoms of the ardent Royalists. They were, it should be admitted, not exactly as loud as the cheers greeting Napoleon as he later passed in review on horseback in the same place.

Beside our unit was a corps of citizen volunteers without uniforms and variously armed, of any rank, any social position and any age. The apparent conviction and dedication of these volunteers was interesting, but compared to the martial air of the soldiers of the old army it was anticipated that they would be of no use against them when put to the test.

The Comte d'Artois, in the uniform of the National Guard, passed in review some of the legions of this guard whose calm and impartial behaviour saved Paris from great disorders in this revolution of the 'Hundred Days'. I was present at one of these reviews in the Place Vendôme. The prince tried to appear confident and smiling, but he must have been very sad in his heart when he met on his way the malicious looks of old soldiers in the middle of the square who were openly speaking anti-Royalist remarks in low voices.

Dismissed by the king after this review, we were assigned to gather at a rendezvous for the next day. On returning to my hotel I found neither Rilliet nor de Vincy who had been ordered to remain in barracks during the day with their respective corps. I was, in fact, not destined to see them again in Paris, for realising themselves abandoned by the rest of the army, the king's household and the court took the road to Ghent in Belgium the following night.

Rilliet followed the royal court to Ghent and then received a mission to join the staff of the allies so that the Bourbon faction could be aware of developments in the forthcoming military operations. In this capacity he was actually present, I believe, at the Battle of Waterloo. As for de Vincy, his corps was dismissed at the frontier and he returned to his home.

Leaving my bed on the 20th March, after having slept the untroubled sleep of the righteous, I was not a little surprised to hear that the king had quit Paris, and that at some point during the day Napoleon was expected to arrive. What a metamorphosis! In the streets, less 'Vive Henri IV' and even less 'Vive Louis XVIII' but 'Vive L'Emperor' was being furiously and universally shouted. No more white cockades were to be seen in the streets, everywhere tricolour cockades were now being worn and then a dense crowd gathered to await Napoleon and his brave men from the Isle of Elba. In a word, the Royalist population of the city had become transformed, as if by magic, into a Bonapartist population.

It was thus seen what weak roots the Bourbons had thrown into France; even those who did not like Bonaparte had not been able to attach themselves to a family which, without protecting any of the interests of their people created by the revolution, seemed to have taken on the task only of resuscitating a forgotten dynasty.

I should have gone back to Geneva because my presence in Paris had been aimless since these events, but I was young, my memories all related to the fortunes and affairs of the Emperor and I found myself in the midst of old comrades who had no qualms about serving Napoleon. I made up my mind not to hurry to leave Paris, to see the turn that things would take, and knowing very well that my hesitation would not be to the taste of my parents, I also took the even less suitable resolution not to hasten to write to them to inform them of my decision.

One fine morning, after more than a fortnight without word from me, I saw Charles Vernes, (the current deputy Governor of the Banque-Parissiene) associate of my friend Dassier who acted on behalf of my family. He was the bearer of a bundle of letters from Geneva, and, moreover, of a verbal argument intending to prove to me, by a thousand good reasons, that I should not embrace such a bad cause as that of Napoleon, which was so poorly viewed in Geneva. I was even more touched by his obliging and moderate tone than by his reasoning. I had already recognised, moreover, that I would cause extreme pain to my parents by taking service under Napoleon. I could no longer turn a deaf ear to the entreaties of those who cared for me and decided at once it was time to take my leave of the French capital.

I resigned as a Marine Artillery officer at the Department of the Navy, after having informed old General Sugny, inspector of that arm under all of the regimes under which it had served, of my motives. Instead of seeing the interesting side of a conscientious step, he received me very badly, making me understand in very unpleasant terms that I was retiring at the moment when my services had become necessary as an imperative.

Be that as it may, a resignation was granted to me on the

20th April, 1815, and I left for Geneva, much saddened to see myself again without a place, and unable even to console myself by the full approbation of my conscience, for I was retiring very unwillingly from a road in which all my natural inclinations propelled me.

I found, having arrived in Geneva, a very different perspective from the scene I had just left. In fact, here was the very opposite position and the whole population was up in arms for fear of Napoleon, whom they roundly hated. Even my brother, Charles, who was a peaceable student of every theology, manoeuvred cannon on the ramparts. Indeed, all of Europe had taken up arms against France.

The day of my return to Geneva was that of the arrival of General de Sonnenberg, appointed commander of the place by the Swiss Confederation. He was received with the greatest demonstrations of joy. In addition to the Geneva Militia, the garrison consisted of a Friborg battalion, a Vaud battalion and a Zurich artillery company. In the staff of the general were Federal Lieutenant-Colonel MM August Bontems, Federal Captain Charles Bontems, Federal Captain Schumacher (today Lucerne state councillor), Kunkler (brother of the Trustee) Federal officer, Serre-Brameral and Masse (Johanny), Cantonal officers.

A few days after my return, I received a visit by Mr August Bontems, who had come to propose to me, on behalf of General de Sonnenberg, the provisional role of Federal Artillery Captain, Assistant to the General Staff. The general did not know me and it was clear that it was Bontems who had indicated me to him, and to whom I owed all the gratitude of this choice. The employment, in the circumstances in which I found myself, was honourable and in pecuniary terms was not to be despised for my fortune was far from being made.

I had, it is true, practically no artillery practice as it applied on land, but by combining my theoretical studies and the habit of military command I hoped to present a passable impression of competence! I knew, moreover, that no one in Geneva understood anything about artillery and I used the proverb '*in the realm of the blind, the one-eyed man is king*' as my justification of suitability for the task in hand. In short, I accepted.

General de Sonnenberg was a rather cold man. He paid very little attention to me, and if I had any complaint of him about anything, it was that I received no precise order from him, and so did not know whether or not he was satisfied with my services. The General Staff of the Federal Artillery, whose headquarters were at Berne, never gave me any sign of life either, so that I can say that I was absolutely delivered to my own inspirations.

In other times we could have taken this letting go for an indication of trust in my abilities, but in reality it was simply the consequence of the infancy of the military institutions in Switzerland at that time. Fortunately, the war did not come to Geneva so my main occupation was to give instruction to the emerging artillery of the Geneva Militia.

A single critical moment signalled this epoch: it was the one in which the French general, Dessaix occupied Carouge with some troops, to make a point on the Chablais. Although he had every intention of respecting Swiss territory (Carouge then belonged to the Sardinian king) there were, however, shots fired by the French patrols from one bank of the Arve to the other. We responded to this display in kind by launching three shells of our own directed at Carouge. The threat of reciprocal action promptly halted hostilities.

CHAPTER-EIGHTEEN

A New Beginning

The news of rout of Napoleon and the French Army at Waterloo, June 18, 1815, and the arrival of an Austrian Army corps commanded by General Frimont, by the Simplon road, decided the intended retreat of the French troops in our vicinity. I attended the signing of the capitulation, at the end of the wooden bridge on the Arve, by virtue of which the province of Carouge was to be evacuated by these troops in the shortest time. The same day Carouge was occupied by the Swiss, and the Austrian Army thereafter traversed Geneva to reach the crossing of the French frontier.

I had a rather curious encounter on one occasion with this Austrian Army. I was going with another officer to Vezenas, on the day when the Austrian column arrived by the Simplon road, when a soldier from this column, marching alone, addressed me in good French, and asked me if I knew a M. Rieu in Geneva. He could not have spoken better and my astonishment was considerable. It happened that this soldier, who held the rank of sergeant-major, had formerly been in the service of France, in the company of my father. I told him where we lived and upon visiting our home, he and my father recognised each other at once.

All fear of invasion and occupation ceased in Geneva. In fact, far from having anything to fear for itself, Geneva had a contingent in the Federal Army and on French territory. My role became useless, and I was thanked for my Federal services, which had lasted about two months. All I had to show for it was a green uniform coat which I then duly handed over to the clerks thus clearing my slate completely.

It was still my saviour, the good lady Trembley de Ribaupierre, who wrote to her friend the Duc d'Escars, returning to France with the Bourbons and still in favour, to restore me to my place which I had resigned under the regime of 'The Hundred Days'. The process succeeded and resulted in a signed letter from the Minister of the Navy, the Vicomte du Bouchage, containing the promise of my re-instatement in the role of a Marine Artillery officer, which was officially confirmed shortly thereafter. I was classified as fully active in the second regiment of Marine Artillery based at Toulon.

In fact, when it came to places, I was embarrassed for choice, for the Council of State of the Canton of Geneva seemed to be very disposed to install me as Captain of the Geneva Company which was to appear in the Swiss regiment of the Royal Guard by virtue of the recently signed capitulation. It is known that the rank of Captain in the Guard was the equivalent of battalion commander in the line.

I did not have to choose as one might think, and we will see why; but if I had to do it, in spite of the temptation to wear a beautiful red coat and thick epaulettes, my inclination would have determined me for the corps where I had my old habits and comrades in arms. The life of the Guard Corps of the Swiss troops seemed rather unattractive to me. Finally, I had so many competitors for the service that I would have shrunk from the idea of making people unhappy.

Cupid, helped by my friend, Dassier, laughed at the Duc d'Escars and the Vicomte du Bouchage and even, Oh irreverence, the State Council of Geneva!

One morning, it was in February 1816, in the midst of my indecision, my dear friend, Dassier, entered my room. He began by making a superb case against military service in peacetime, then followed it with an eloquent plea on the sweetness of marriage and civil life, and, in conclusion pointed out to me that I was dancing a lot with a certain young lady, Marie Lasserre, whom I did not seem to displease. He went on to propose that a match with this young lady would be, if I were approved, a fine one for a man whose only fortune was a severed thumb and a scar on his forehead. Furthermore, that he knew her father a little personally, and finally, if I did not oppose him, he would go forthwith and ask him for the hand of his daughter on my behalf. His eloquence, which only encouraged my own secret desires, which the natural reserve would ensure would never have been brought to light without this invitation, had no difficulty in persuading me to concur.

No sooner was the matter said than it was done. My learned parents did not, as we thought, have any objection to make, and that very day I was certain that a request in form would be received. Never was an important affair more quickly arranged, and never was the surprise of my other friends and relatives, on hearing such a quick issue, never more legitimate.

I made a marriage of a different nature with the Republic, taking the position of auditor. Everything then was impromptu for me, for I was as unprepared for this Civil Magistracy as I would have been to be appointed a Bishop or the Pope. In short, to give an idea of my accuracy in making the dates coincide, I will say that I entered into the duties of my position of auditor on April 15, 1816, and that I was married at the church of Chêne-Bougeries the next day, April 16, 1816.

Here begins the part of my life spent before the eyes of my citizens, and therefore better known than the one I have just spoken of. The second part also had its tribulations, but the pleasures with which they have been intermingled, the feeling of being useful to my country and the signs of approval that have kindly been given to me, have been for me a sweet compensation; more than a compensation, since I found happiness there, as much as we can find it here on earth.

Today, the superficial that was outside, in this happiness, is over for me. Separated by the infirmity of my hearing from public affairs, I am no more than a useless member of society. May I work for my inner happiness by triumphing over anxiety, impatience, selfishness and lack of goodwill and charity in my character, by contributing to the happiness of my surroundings, by making my peace with my conscience and, above all, with God, who has always granted me a protection of which I can only be worthy by my gratitude and my spiritual improvement.

A Short History of the Marine Artillery—1795-1815

THE EARLY DAYS

Following several failed experiments concerning the structure of manning its navy, the French Government, in 1795, decided upon the creation of seven demi-brigades of Marine Artillery. Each was to be composed of three battalions of nine companies with each company having 120 men. This force of over 22,000 men was to be positioned on the coast of France distributed in the following locations:—

Three demi-brigades stationed in Brest, Two demi-brigades stationed at Toulon and one demi-brigade at L'orient and Rochefort respectively.

This initiative marked, for a period of time, a consistent approach to the garrisoning of ships of war and to the servicing of their guns, for despite the specific nature of the unit title, the Marine Artillery was charged with undertaking both functions.

In its capacity as being the military element on board ships as opposed to a maritime element principally concerned with their sailing, the Marine Artillery were organised and equipped in the manner of infantry regiments, though equally they were required to operate as artillerymen as the occasion required. This would apply to actions fought at sea, but the brigades were also charged with garrison duties at ports and the manning of coastal fortifications. This arrangement applied consistently from the brigade's inception until 1813 when losses among the army necessitated the removal of the majority of the personnel of the

Marine Artillery from their traditional functions and their employment during a land-based campaign in Germany.

Towards the end of the 18th century and during the first years of the 19th century, the Marine Artillery served in 1796 during the expedition to Ireland, where they were employed as crews on several ships- a necessity provoked by a shortage of sailors. Then two years later in 1798, it served with the 'Legion Nautique' following the Battle of Aboukir during the ill-fated Egyptian Campaign. 1801 saw sixteen companies of the Marine Artillery employed as 'Grenadiers' in Italy while in the following year as the global conflict embraced the islands of the West Indies, the brigades saw action on Santo Domingo, Martinque and Guadaloupe.

Fundamental changes came in 1803 when the demi-brigades were abolished and the Marine Artillery was re-organised into four regiments comprised of twelve battalions in total. The First and Second Regiments, Marine Artillery had four battalions each, whilst the Third and Fourth Regiments had two battalions each. These battalions were made up of six companies each of 200 men making a total of 14,400 effectives, all of whom were volunteers.

In 1805, a fifth battalion was added to the Second Regiment, Marine Artillery. At this time the regiments were distributed thus:

First Regiment, 4 battalions at Brest

Second Regiment, 5 battalions—1 at Genoa, 2 at Brest, 2 at Toulon

Third Regiment, 2 battalions at Rochefort

Fourth Regiment, 2 battalions at L'orient

In December 1806 a change in recruitment policy meant that conscription was introduced in the same manner as it was applied for admissions to the French Army. The Marine Artillery regiments served at The Battle of Trafalgar in 1805, between 1806-1808 once more in the West Indies on Guadaloupe and Santo Domingo, in Portugal between 1807-1808, where they were employed in the refitting of Portuguese ships, in 1811 at

Flushing in the Netherlands and between 1811–1814 during the Peninsular War in Spain where three officers and 120 men served as conventional artillery during the land based campaign. Additionally, detached officers served in Java, Spain and in Russia.

The progressive dominance of the Royal Navy at sea during this time ensured that the French Navy remained substantially blockaded in its own ports, which meant that the Marine Artillery entered into a period of inactivity. Men were either established on ships of war at anchor or languishing as garrisons in coastal forts and ports.

In 1812 another reorganisation meant that the regiments now featured companies with a complement of 250 men. The newly titled, 'Corps Imperial de L'Artillerie de la Marine' was at this point 19,500 men strong and was distributed as follows:

First Regiment at Brest

Second Regiment 1 battalion each at Genoa, Rochefort and L'orient. 2 battalions in Toulon

Third Regiment at Cherbourg

Fourth Regiment at Antwerp.

THE CAMPAIGN OF 1813

Following the destruction of the *Grande Armée* during the Russian Campaign of 1812 which naturally substantially depleted the ranks of the infantry, Napoleon transferred the four regiments of the Marine Artillery from their traditional duties within the navy to the army where they were, despite the misnomer, to be employed as infantry.

Originally it was intended to double the number of battalions of the Marine Artillery to twenty-four, each comprising 840 men which in turn would increase the size of the force to 20,000. As it transpired there were insufficient men available to realise this plan and so the Minister of War, General Clarke, was instructed make up the numbers with 2,000 conscripts from the 'levy of the four classes'. These were young men aged 20–24 years who had not been drafted between 1809–1812. A further

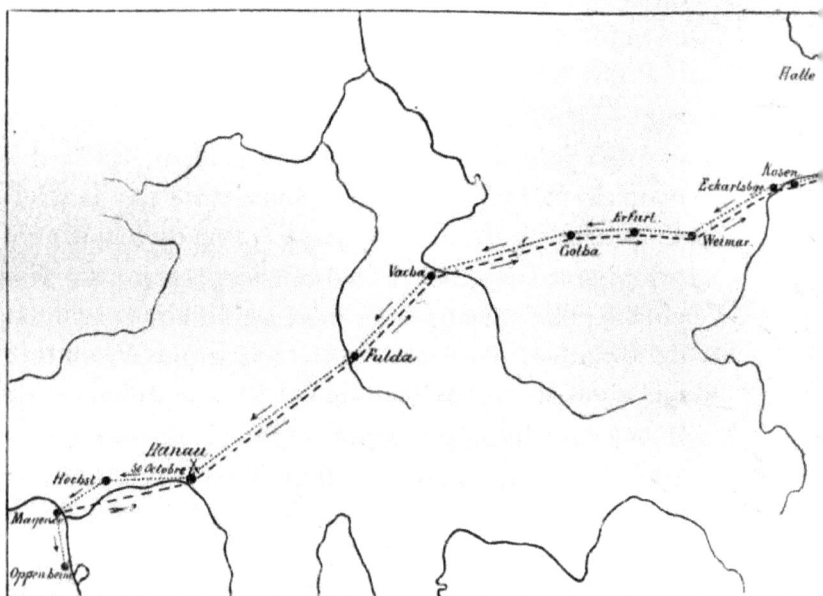

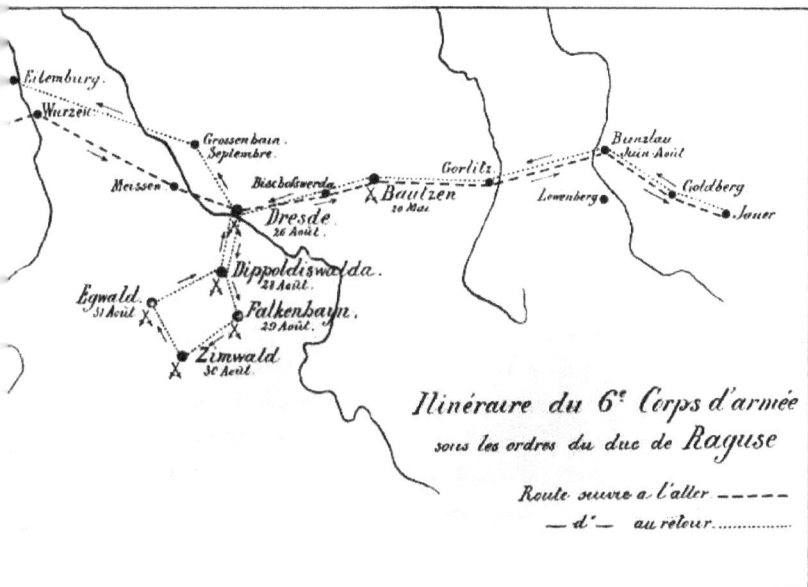

Itinéraire du 6ᵉ Corps d'armée
sous les ordres du duc de Raguse

Route suivie a l'aller _ _ _ _ _
_ dᵒ _ au retour ....

2,000 young men, aged 18-19 years from the conscription of 1814 were added to this number.

Despite this injection there remained a shortfall of personnel required to realise the intended target number of battalions and accordingly that number was reduced to twenty.

The Marine Artillery recalled its detachments and mustered in Brest (First Regiment), Toulon (Second Regiment), Cherbourg (Third Regiment) and Antwerp (Anvers by its old French name) (Fourth Regiment). Each battalion had six companies, each of three officers and 137 men. With the addition of the staff this meant each battalion contained 844 men.

The regiments were issued with blue greatcoats which, when they were worn, gave those who saw the ranks at distance the impression that they were part of the Imperial Guard. The men were also issued three pairs of shoes and ordered to march to Mayence to form part of what became VI Corps under the command of Marshal Marmont. Upon arrival at their destination, Marmont complained that he not been given the number of men that he had been promised. In this accusation he was correct for the French Navy had withheld a quantity of the men destined for his command to man the port batteries. Although Clarke, the Minister of War, was well aware of this shortfall and the reasons for it Napoleon remained ignorant of the fact, though when the matter finally came to light he found himself in agreement with the decision and injected more conscripts to make up the missing numbers.

Nevertheless, the battalions remained under normal strength and this issue was resolved by the creation—from the resources available—of fourteen 'war' battalions whilst six battalions would remain as cadres in Mayence.

The fourteen battalions that marched with Marmont's force therefore averaged 691 men each.

First Regiment—4 battalions and the Third Regiment—2 battalions, formed the First Brigade under Cacault and were part of General Compans' 20th Division whilst the Second Regiment of 6 battalions and the Fourth Regiment of 2 battalions became the First Brigade under Buquet in the 21st Division under Bonnet.

Marmont was originally sceptical of the value of the Marine Artillery. He believed the men were good material, but that their officers had grown old in the service and had been too used to long periods of inactivity. There is no doubt that these hastily formed units lacked much in the way of equipment that established regiments of infantry might expect as regular. They suffered in shortages of fundamentals including cartridge boxes, breeches, good quality muskets and even drums. Surgeons were likewise wanting.

Marmont was soon to review his doubts, writing, 'the regiments of the Naval Artillery act superbly and inspire the conscripts'. It was at this point that the principal character of this book, Jean Louis Rieu joined the campaign and so that period is related here in more detail.

The First Regiment in Brest was increased from four battalions to eight. Its headquarters staff was made up of a colonel, a major and two majors *en second,* chosen from among the battalion heads who had distinguished themselves and served in the army. Each battalion had at its headquarters staff one *chef de bataillon,* one adjutant-major and two non-commissioned adjutants. It was made up of six companies. Each company had one captain, lieutenant, one sub-lieutenant and 137 men, giving a total of 844 men per battalion previously indicated.

The officer cadres of the twenty-four new companies of the First Regiment were composed of the captains *en second* and lieutenant *en second* who were promoted to lieutenants *en premier.* As for the 48 sub-lieutenants necessary, they were taken from the military school of Saint-Cyr, from Vélites' infantry of the Guard and NCOs of naval artillery who had campaigned on land.

The Second, Third and Fourth Regiments also had the number of their battalions doubled, as a result of which the Second Regiment was brought up to ten battalions and the other two to four. They had the same organisation as the First Regiment.

The first six battalions of the First Regiment were directed to Mayence, together with the first eight of the Second and the first three of the Third and Fourth, in all twenty battalions with a complement of 16,895 men. The six other battalions were required to stay in their depots and be completed by means of conscription.

In Mayence, the 20 battalions were reviewed by the Duc de Valmy who was tasked with completing their training.

The minister for the navy was authorised to keep 500 gunners of the naval artillery for the needs of the fleet. These men were placed after the regiments and recorded on a particular roll.

The twenty battalions of war were designated to form the Second Division of the Second Observation Corps of the Rhine.

Malaize says:

> The disembarkation of the Marine Artillery, caused a great sensation in the fleet. It gave rise to the strongest representations from the admirals commanding the squadrons of l'Escaut (The Scheldt) and the Mediterranean, who stated formally that they could do nothing without them.

The 500 men left in the navy were chosen from among the best chief gunners; garrisoning the vessels was given to sailors of the guard.

BATTLE OF LÜTZEN

The Naval Artillery arrived at Mayence in the middle of March, forming part of the VI Army Corps, commanded by Marshal Marmont, Duc de Raguse.

The First Regiment, commanded by Colonel Emond, was made up of 3,338 men in six battalions. The Second Regiment, that of Colonel Buquet, had 3,310 men in eight battalions. The Third Regiment, under Colonel Butraud formed 1,476 men in three battalions. Finally, the Fourth Regiment, under the command of Colonel Rouvroy, had a strength of three battalions and 1,516 men.

This gave a total of 9,640 men, the actual strength ready for battle. The First and Third regiments formed the Cacault bri-

BATTLE OF LÜTZEN

C. Röchling.

gade of the First Division (20th), commanded by General Compans. The Second and Fourth regiments made up the Buquet brigade of the Second Division (21st), under General Bonnet.

In his report to the headquarters of the *Grande Armée*, the Duc de Raguse gave the following account of the involvement of the 6th corps at the Battle of Lützen (May 2, 1813):

> I was strongly entrenched in the village of Starfield (Starsiedel) which was to be my strong point. I sent the Compans division forward from the village and a little to the left.
>
> At this, the enemy mustered a large force against me, and in particular a good deal of artillery. More than 150 cannon were directed against my single army corps; but the troops stood up calmly to the fire and with a courage that deserves the highest praise. The Compans division, in particular, being the most exposed, deserves special praise and its ranks, constantly thinned, were reformed with cries of *'Vive l'Empereur!'*
>
> Immediately after this terrible gunfire, the enemy cavalry set off and made a fierce charge, also directed against the First Regiment of Naval Artillery. This excellent regiment, commanded by the brave Colonel Emond, showed at that moment what good infantry can achieve against cavalry and the enemy's efforts failed against its bayonets. Other charges were made and all equally without success.
>
> The enemy, thinking that after the exhaustion of such a long day, the soldiers would be lying down and their weapons in their holsters, arrived at ten o'clock with four regiments of *élite* cavalry. These four regiments charged among us with extraordinary verve, but found every man at his post. All orders given were carried out to the letter and the enemy surrounded our squares with his dead, without breaking one of them. Three hundred hussars remained on the field and reports by the Prussians said that the guard regiment was entirely destroyed.
>
> This was the end of a fine day. It was the Sixth army

corps that had the honour, in this memorable campaign, of firing the first cannon shots and the last gunshots. I cannot praise highly enough the troops with whose command His Majesty has entrusted me. The naval soldiers have shown themselves worthy of the army to which His Majesty has attached them.

In addition to this, one can read in the *Intimate Memoirs of the Time of the Empire,* by Marco de Saint-Hilaire, on the subject of the Battle of Lützen:

The corps of the Duc de Raguse having entered in line on the right, the cavalry, that the enemy thought it could throw into the plain of Lützen, was suddenly halted in the village of Starzieldel (Starsiedel) by the Naval Division of Compans, a general of the highest merit, as Napoleon well described him. It formed its squares which become so many redoubts, and it was against these walls of men that seven charges of 25,000 cavalry were broken, being unable to breach them.

According to the *Moniteur* on May 9, the naval regiments "covered the battlefield with the *élite* of the enemy cavalry."

Our losses were considerable. The 1st regiment, in particular, suffered a great deal, with 742 killed and 350 wounded, meaning that a third of its strength was put out of action. The disproportion between the figure for those killed and those wounded is explained by the long and savage cannon-fire that the regiment had to suffer at the start of the day, which it bore without giving way. It was doubtless thinking of this that the Duc de Raguse wrote in his *Memoirs:*

The naval artillery regiments, making up the core of my army corps, deserved much praise for their daring and their morale. Never did soldiers expose themselves so readily to enemy cannon-fire or stay under it with such fortitude.

As for the Allies, facing such heroic determination and vigor-

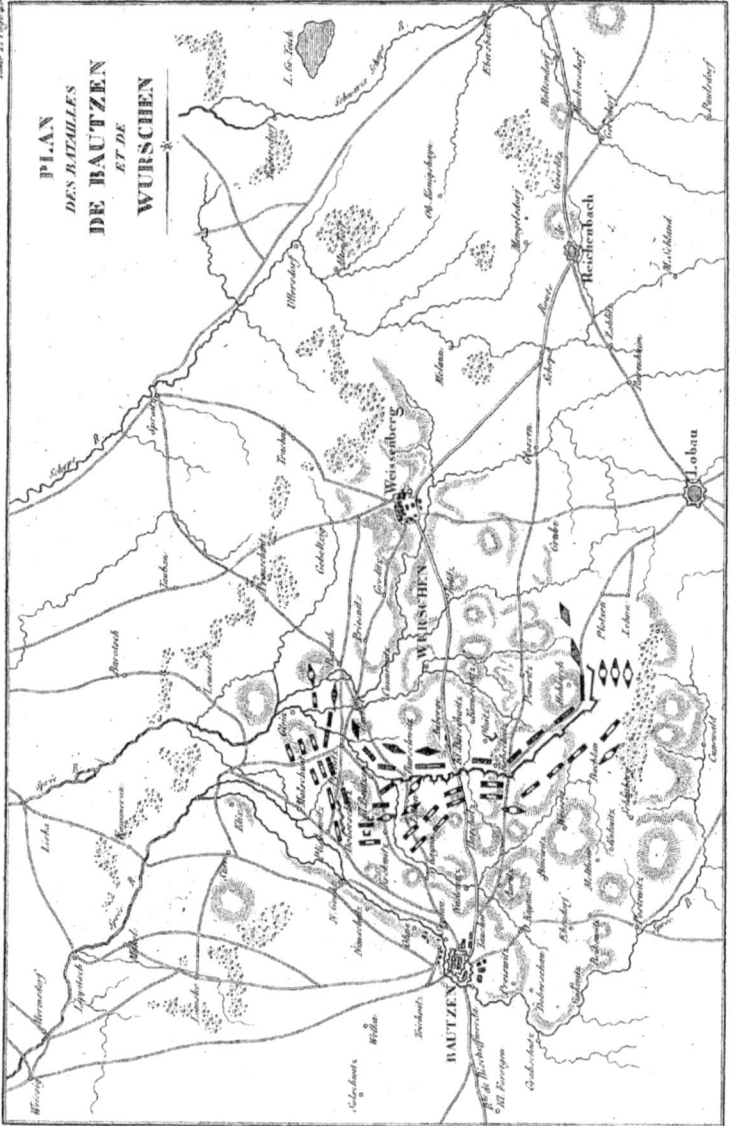

PLAN
DES BATAILLES
DE BAUTZEN
ET DE
WURSCHEN

ous resistance and also mistaking the long blue coats worn by the naval artillery they thought they were dealing with the remains of the Old Guard who had escaped the disaster of Moscow.

BATTLES OF BAUTZEN AND WURSCHEN

This is how the Duc de Raguse sums up the day of May 20, 1813 (Bautzen) in a letter written to the chief of staff on the field of battle at half past eleven in the evening:

> I shall say no more than that we have everywhere over-thrown the enemy, that the Bonnet division and its general have performed wonderfully well, and that the troops of His Majesty entrusted to my command deserved the highest praise, especially the 37th Light and the 4th Naval.

The Marshal also says in his *Memoirs:*

> As Bautzen continued to defend itself and prevented the advance of the 11th corps, I detached the first division under General Compans to take the town from the rear. The battery defending the approaches was seized at the double and the ramparts scaled. All the Russian soldiers in the town were taken prisoner.

As for the day of May 21 (Wurschen), we can quote the following passage from the *Moniteur:*

> On May 21, at eleven o'clock in the morning, the Duc de Raguse marched 1000 *toises* (circa 2000 metres) forward from his position and came under dreadful cannon-fire in front of the redoubts and all the enemy entrenchments.
> At seven in the evening, the Prince de la Moskowa and General Lauriston arrived at Wurtchen (Wurschen). The Duc de Raguse got the order to make the opposite move-ment from that made by the Guard and occupied all the entrenched villages and all the redoubts that the enemy was obliged to evacuate, and advanced in the direction of Hochkirch, thus taking the whole of the enemy's left by a flanking movement, which caused a terrible confusion

BATTLE OF WURSCHEN

among them.

On the days of May 20 and 21, the First Naval Artillery Regiment lost 226 killed and 322 wounded out of a total of around 2000 men. The Second Regiment had 59 killed and 136 wounded.

Colonels Emond of the 1st Regiment and Butraud of the 3rd were promoted generals and appointed to serve in the 14th corps. Brave Emond, who had been seriously wounded at Lützen, would not survive his wounds; he died on December 26, 1813, after a life given entirely to military glory.

Colonel Falba who, at Lützen, had commanded the 1st Regiment and the brigade after Colonel Emond and General Cacault were put out of action, was nominated to go to Holland and take up command of the 4th Foreign Regiment.

After the bloody battles of Lützen and Bautzen, 500 naval artillery were seconded to the Artillery of the Guard to fill the places left vacant and several officers of the naval artillery also passed into this *élite* corps, among others the *chef de bataillon* de Coisy who had command of a division of horse artillery.

Following the reduction in their numbers, the regiments of Naval Artillery were reduced, the First to four battalions, the Second to six battalions, the Third and Fourth to two battalions.

During the armistice, the ports sent large detachments and moreover one battalion per regiment (that is, four battalions) came to reinforce the troops of Naval Artillery in Saxony, so only two battalions were left in France, one in Brest, the other in Toulon.

On August 17, when the armistice was broken, the regiments of Naval Artillery were made up as follows:

First Regiment: 5 battalions, 2930 combatants.

Second Regiment: 7 battalions, 3372 combatants;

Third Regiment: 3 battalions, 2197 combatants;

Fourth Regiment: 3 battalions, 2014 combatants

Total strength: 10513 men.

Battle of DRESDEN.
Morning of the
2nd. Day.

French. Allies.

Willsdruff

English Miles.
0 1 2 3 4 5

R. ELBE

DRESDEN

Pillnitz

DeBna

Friedrichstadt

Strehlen

RUSSIAN·S·AND

PRUSS·RUSSIAN

AUSTR

N·WEISSERITZ

Tharandt

SCHWARTZENBERG'S
MARCH ON DRESDEN.
English Miles
0 5 10 15

Dresden

R. Elbe

Pirna

Königstein

Dippoldiswalde

Guttleba

Altenberg

George

Toplitz

BOHEMIA

ERZ GEBIRGE

SAXONY

Freiberg

Marienberg

DIPPOLDISWALDE

These troops were distributed as follows in the Sixth Corps:

The First Regiment, commanded by Major Deschamps, was part of the 1st brigade (Pelleport) of the 1st division (Compans). The Third Regiment belonged to the 2nd brigade (Joubert) of the same division. The Fourth Regiment, Colonel Rouvroy, was part of the 1st brigade (Jamin) of the 2nd division (Lagrange) and the Second Regiment, Colonel Deschamps, by itself made up the 2nd brigade (Buquet) of that division

After the Battle of Dresden, on August 26, in which its *avant-garde* was involved in several skirmishes that bore witness to "the intrepidity of its troops" (the *Moniteur*), the 6th corps was given the order to pursue the enemy. The Duc de Raguse carried out this mission without rest or pause, attacking every day for a new battle (27th, 28th, 29th, 30th and 31st of August).

BATTLE OF DIPPOLDISWALDA (AUGUST 28)

Marmont describes this engagement as follows:

I must in this circumstance give the troops the praise that they have so well deserved. They fought against superior forces and against the enemy's best troops and they drove them back despite the obstacles of the ground which were designed to favour the enemy's resistance. I must in particular praise General Lagrange and General Compans; the 32nd Light, the 1st and 4th Naval regiments and the 37th Light deserve particular mention. I must name Sergeant Pujol of the 4th Naval Regiment who, already twice wounded by gunfire and attacked by thirty Russians simultaneously, launched an attack against them with three men of his regiment and took them all prisoner. (*Operational Journal of the 6th corps* by the Duc de Raguse; War Archives).

ENGAGEMENT AT FALKENHEIM (AUGUST 29)

The report on this affair contains the following passages:

I gave the order to General Lagrange to attack the enemy. Despite very stiff resistance on their part, the valour of our troops was such that in a moment everything was overturned and the enemy pursued as far as the entry to the pass where he left many artillery pieces and carriages. Only nightfall stopped us in our pursuit.

The 37th Light, the 4th Naval and one battalion of the Second Naval, commanded by the head of battalion, Durand, an officer of the highest distinction, covered themselves in glory. The enthusiasm of the troops was such that I needed to exert my authority to moderate it, in order to make its effects more certain by only using combined efforts and not leaving to chance a success that was certain with such troops.

In this engagement, Sergeant Martin of the 4th Naval Regiment, seeing his wounded captain being carried off by the enemy, charged those who were taking him single-handed and freed him. *(Operational Journal of the 6th corps* by the Duc de Raguse; War Archives).

ENGAGEMENTS AT ZINNWALD AND EGWALD (30 AND 31 AUGUST).

Writing about the fight at Zinnwald, the Duc de Raguse expresses himself in the following terms:

And this division (Lagrange), after marching vigorously, at the same time as that of General Compans, came out with the greatest resolve. The enemy was driven back on all fronts, pursued with swords at his back and thrown into the dreadful passes and down the precipices that one finds in Zinnwald and Toeplitz. (*Operational Journal of the 6th corps* by the Duc de Raguse; War Archives).

At the news of the defeat of Vandamme, the 6th corps returned to the rear, after fighting again at Egwald on August 31. Marmont ends the journal of his operations in Bohemia with the following passage:

On September 10 in the morning, I arrived in Dresden where I had orders to occupy the town and the entrenched camp and to rest my troops there.

The 6th army corps had thus marched for twenty-two days in succession, without a single pause, fought in a variety of circumstances and made marches of twelve leagues. But morale was so good and the enthusiasm so general, that except for the wounded and a very small number of men who had stayed behind, the corps were still intact and not a single artillery carriage or wagon or supplies had been lost or even stayed behind.

In these different engagements, the 1st Naval Artillery Regiment was the one that suffered the greatest number or losses: it had 191 killed and 227 wounded.

BATTLE OF LEIPZIG

We shall once more turn to the Duc de Raguse for an account of the struggles of the 6th corps in Leipzig. On October 16, this corps was fighting alone at Möckern, in front of Leipzig.

The enemy was approaching rapidly, its forces seemed to be coming up out of the ground and multiplying in front of our eyes: it was all the army of Silesia.

The enemy attack was first directed against the village of Moeckern (Möckern); this village was attacked fiercely and the enemy withstood all my artillery fire. It was defended in the same way by the troops of the 2nd division under General Lagrange. The Second Naval Artillery Regiment, which was entrusted with the defence of this post, combined vigour and tenacity. It preserved the village for a long time, losing it and retaking it several times, but the enemy redoubled his efforts and sent in powerful auxiliaries, concerned only with this point.

At that, I ordered a change of oblique front by brigade, which immediately formed six lines in echelon which were equally well placed to support the village where all the battle seemed to be taking place. The 37th Light and the Fourth Marine Regiment were sent in succession to the village; they took it and defended it with all the cour-

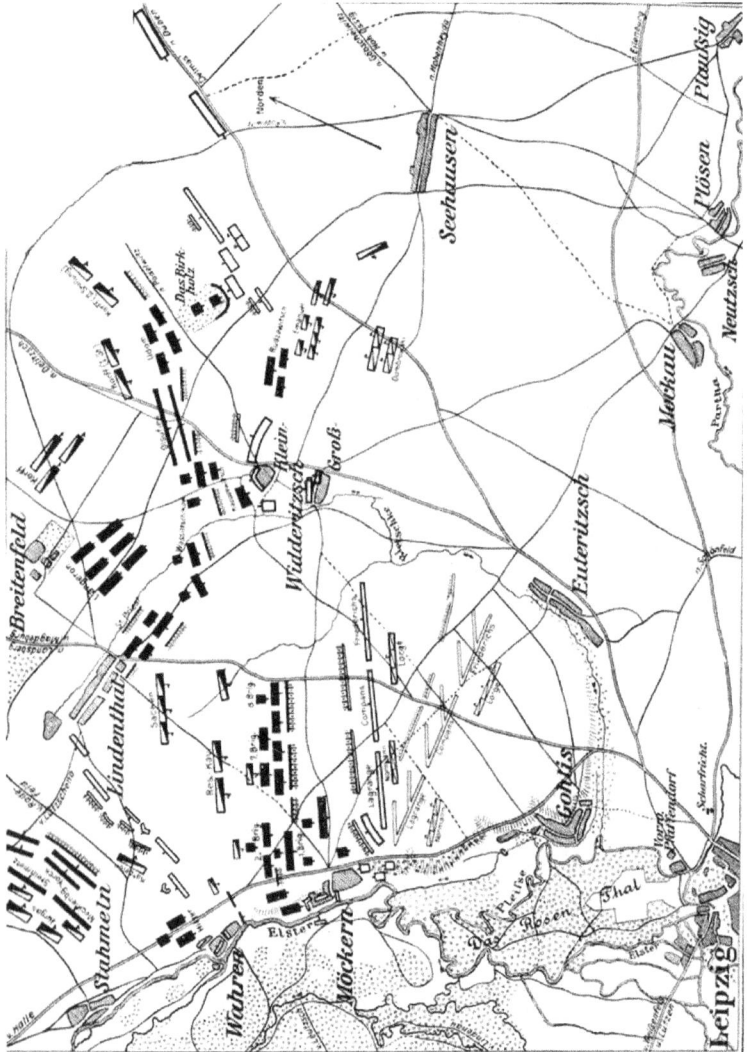

Battle of Möckern, 16th October, 1813

age that one might expect from such good troops.

The battle had been continuing with the same relentless fury for more than three hours and the enemy had suffered huge losses because of the advantage over its massed attacks enjoyed by the position of our artillery; but new forces kept coming up and renewing the attack. The simultaneous explosion of four caissons out of 12 momentarily halted the fire of one of our main batteries and, at that moment, the enemy made a decisive charge. I then engaged a part of the troops of the First Division who were forming the echelons of the centre to support the troops already engaged in battle and combat the enemy who was making a movement from his centre.

The battle took on a new character and our infantry found itself, in a moment, only twenty yards from the enemy. Never was there a fiercer engagement. In a few moments, I was myself wounded and everyone around me dead or stricken.

It was in this situation that the enemy made a furious cavalry charge in which several battalions belonging to the First and Third Regiments of Marine Artillery were literally crushed. None the less, they continued to fight without retreating until nightfall, then returned to the rear. The next day, October 18, (actually it was 2 days later), the 6th corps, supported by the 3rd, had to confront the Silesian Army, to which was joined the Swedish Army.

The enemy deployed 150 cannon at the same time as it attacked the village of Schoenfeld with the greatest resolve. Seven times, the enemy managed to seize the greater part of the village and seven times it was driven out again. It was once more the 2nd Division commanded by General Lagrange and a detachment of the 3rd which had the glory of defending this village and never did troops behave in a more heroic manner, taking no account of the number of the enemy.

LEIPZIG.
The First Day's Battle.
Positions at 9.a.m.
Oct. 16. 1813.

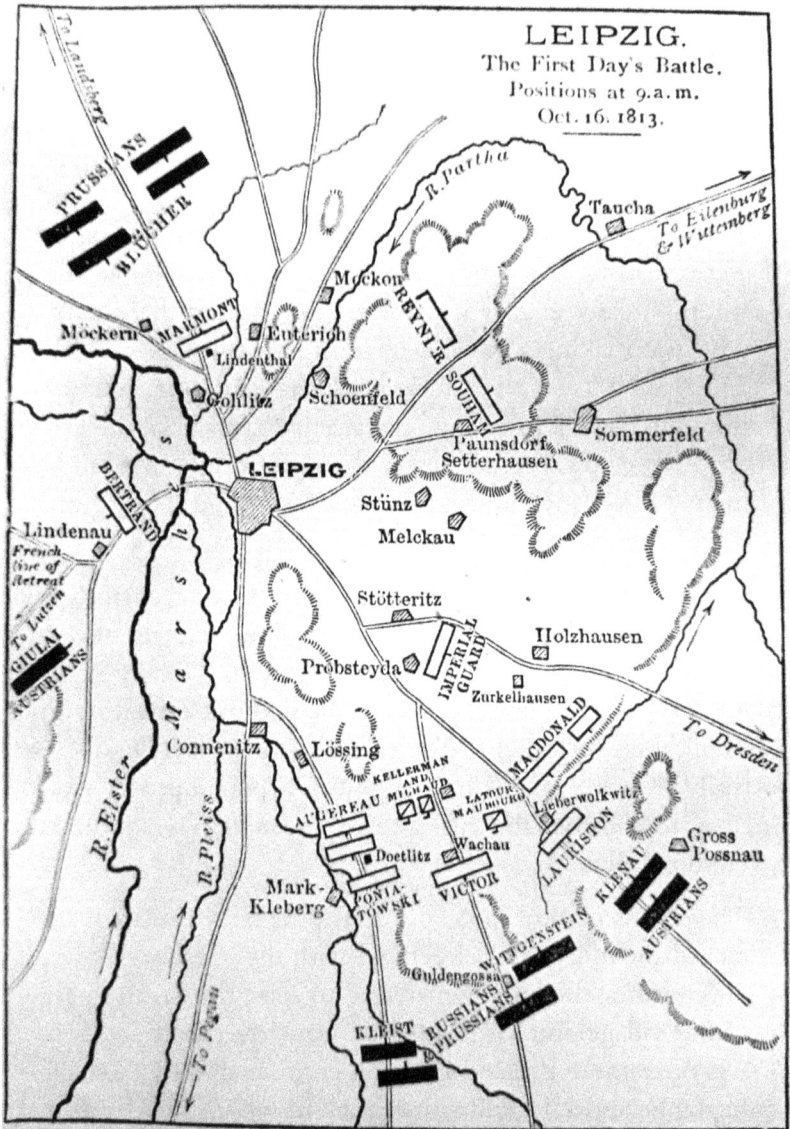

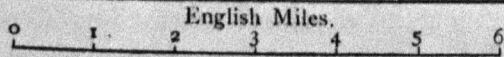

I know of no praise too high for such brave and devoted troops who, despite the losses that they had suffered two days earlier, fought with no less courage.

Among the men who distinguished themselves that day, I must mention Sergeant Dumont of the 4th Naval Regiment who, attacked simultaneously by four enemy infantrymen (*tirailleurs*) who ordered him to surrender, charged them with a bayonet, killed two and forced the others to surrender and took them prisoner to his battalion, as evidence of his fine action.

On the following day, the 19th, the Sixth Corps had to defend the Faubourg de la Halle in Leipzig.

During the retreat, after this corps had crossed the Elster, the bridge was cut before all the French Army had reached the opposite shore. The Duc de Raguse drew up his troops along the river and covered the crossing of those who swam or took a small bridge which they had managed to construct.

The losses of the Naval Artillery, in these different battles, were huge: The First regiment lost 1,420 men and the second 1,178.

BATTLE OF HANAU

On October 24, the 6th corps was crossing Erfurth and left there 350 naval artillerymen of the First Regiment and 734 of the Second to hold the position. There were already 300 men in the town from the same service who had just arrived from Cherbourg and had not yet had time to join the army in Leipzig. We know that subsequently the garrison at Erfurt was so weak that it retired into the fortress of Petersberg, under the convention of December 20, 1813.

On October 30, the 6th corps was in battle at Hanau. Marmont says:

At four in the evening, dispatched by successive order and a heavy sound of cannon fire that I could hear from the direction of Hanau, I arrived at the head of my column and immediately joined the battle. A vigorous charge with bayonets by 600 men, at the head of whom were General

The attack of the Brandenburg Hussars at Möckern

Lagrange and General Jamin, was enough to free our left flank and drive back the enemy who had gathered a lot of men at that point to cover his retreat. Night prevented us from pursuing him.

On the following day, the Duc de Raguse, with the help of some bombs, evacuated the town of Hanau, then charged and drove back the Austrian and Bavarian forces, which ensured the safe passage of the river by the French Army.

In the battles of Hanau, the 2nd Naval Artillery regiment had 114 men put out of action.

★★★★★★

On November 2, the 6th corps recrossed the Rhine at Mayence and had to bear the onslaught of a cruel epidemic (typhus).

According to Thiers, it was the Second Naval Artillery Regiment that was the more stricken by the illness.

The battalion of military workmen (sappers?) of Spain, all of whose officers belonged to the Naval Artillery, had been brought in to join the *Grande Armée*. It arrived at Mayence on April 30 1813, crossed the Rhine on June 10, and was in Dresden on the 30th of the same month. It worked on the fortifications of that town and participated in the various engagements that subsequently took place there. After the Battle of Leipzig, it was sent to Torgau and took part in the defence of that town.

A certain number of naval artillery officers were used, in 1813-1814, in defence of positions: apart from Erfuth and Torgau, they were in Dresden, Danzig, Antwerp, Mayence, Genoa, etc.

★★★★★★

Among the officers of the naval artillery who distinguished themselves in the 1813 campaign, we may mention:

L'Elen, Captain. In the Battle of Dresden, this officer picked up and carried outside the artillery emplacement a burning shell fired by the enemy battery.

Pussin, Lieutenant: cited in despatches on October 18, for his outstanding conduct.

La Prairie, Captain. In and around Gotha, during the retreat, he led 25 men in resistance, preventing a column of 1,200 enemy soldiers from crossing a bridge. On October 27, with 60 men, he opened the way in front of Hanau and so contributed to saving a great part of the equipment and more than 3,000 wounded and others who were walking alone.

Finally, Colonel Falba who, in Holland, seized the fortified stronghold of Woorden and commanded it during the siege that it had to sustain.

LOSSES OF THE NAVAL ARTILLERY

The lists concern the losses suffered by the naval artillery during the 1813 campaign, according to documents in the Ministry of War.

MEN

	Sent to Germany	Killed	In German Hospitals	Prisoners or left behind
Reg. 1st	5357	1166	2271	815
Reg. 2nd	5588	635	2058	64
Reg. 3rd	2753	324	1360	366
Reg. 4th	3640	287	1602	1074
Total	17338	2412	7291	2319

	Moved to Guards Art.	Left in Erfurth	Strength Nov 2 1813
Reg. 1st	198	350	557
Reg. 2nd	200 (?)	734	1897
Reg. 3rd	71	—	632
Reg. 4th	102	—	575
Total	571	1084	3661

OFFICERS

The losses of officers for the First Regiment have not been established, but it is certain that they were far above those of the other regiments.

Reg.	Killed or died	Died of illness	Wounded left on battlefield or in hospital	Prisoners
2nd	33	2	14	2
3rd	19	1	5	4
4th	12	3	4	8
Total	64	6	23	14

It has not been possible to know the names of all the officers killed or wounded during the campaign; in particular, almost nothing has been found out about the sub-lieutenants from Saint-Cyr and the NCOs. The only information that has been found concern only a certain number of officers who were serving in the naval artillery before 1813. The lists are therefore very incomplete, as from the fact that there are only the names of 22 officers killed or died of wounds, when the true figure should be in the region of 100.

1814

By this point the Allied armies invaded France. The Marine Artillery was sorely depleted by all of its hard-fought engagements, but still remained a component of Marmont's VI Corps. The unit fought again at Vauchamps, Champaubert, Montmiral and in the battle for Paris. At the cessation of hostilities on 5th May, 1814 there remained only 695 effectives.

As all know, Napoleon abdicated, was sent to the Mediterranean island of Elba, but took his chance, as he inevitably was bound to do, and escaped. So began his last great gamble for power. The Marine Artillery rallied to his call to arms and were employed in four auxiliary foot artillery companies attached to the Middle and Young Guard and in an auxiliary horse artillery battery attached to the VI Army Corps. All these troops took part in the last great engagement of the era at Waterloo in 1815.

LEONAUR

ALSO FROM LEONAUR
AVAILABLE IN SOFTCOVER OR HARDCOVER WITH DUST JACKET

THE FALL OF THE MOGHUL EMPIRE OF HINDUSTAN *by H. G. Keene*—By the beginning of the nineteenth century, as British and Indian armies under Lake and Wellesley dominated the scene, a little over half a century of conflict brought the Moghul Empire to its knees.

LADY SALE'S AFGHANISTAN *by Florentia Sale*—An Indomitable Victorian Lady's Account of the Retreat from Kabul During the First Afghan War.

THE CAMPAIGN OF MAGENTA AND SOLFERINO 1859 *by Harold Carmichael Wylly*—The Decisive Conflict for the Unification of Italy.

FRENCH'S CAVALRY CAMPAIGN *by J. G. Maydon*—A Special Correspondent's View of British Army Mounted Troops During the Boer War.

CAVALRY AT WATERLOO *by Sir Evelyn Wood*—British Mounted Troops During the Campaign of 1815.

THE SUBALTERN *by George Robert Gleig*—The Experiences of an Officer of the 85th Light Infantry During the Peninsular War.

NAPOLEON AT BAY, 1814 *by F. Loraine Petre*—The Campaigns to the Fall of the First Empire.

NAPOLEON AND THE CAMPAIGN OF 1806 *by Colonel Vachée*—The Napoleonic Method of Organisation and Command to the Battles of Jena & Auerstädt.

THE COMPLETE ADVENTURES IN THE CONNAUGHT RANGERS *by William Grattan*—The 88th Regiment during the Napoleonic Wars by a Serving Officer.

BUGLER AND OFFICER OF THE RIFLES *by William Green & Harry Smith*—With the 95th (Rifles) during the Peninsular & Waterloo Campaigns of the Napoleonic Wars.

NAPOLEONIC WAR STORIES *by Sir Arthur Quiller-Couch*—Tales of soldiers, spies, battles & sieges from the Peninsular & Waterloo campaingns.

CAPTAIN OF THE 95TH (RIFLES) *by Jonathan Leach*—An officer of Wellington's sharpshooters during the Peninsular, South of France and Waterloo campaigns of the Napoleonic wars.

RIFLEMAN COSTELLO *by Edward Costello*—The adventures of a soldier of the 95th (Rifles) in the Peninsular & Waterloo Campaigns of the Napoleonic wars.

LEONAUR

ALSO FROM LEONAUR
AVAILABLE IN SOFTCOVER OR HARDCOVER WITH DUST JACKET

OFFICERS & GENTLEMEN *by Peter Hawker & William Graham*—Two Accounts of British Officers During the Peninsula War: Officer of Light Dragoons by Peter Hawker & Campaign in Portugal and Spain by William Graham .

THE WALCHEREN EXPEDITION *by Anonymous*—The Experiences of a British Officer of the 81st Regt. During the Campaign in the Low Countries of 1809.

LADIES OF WATERLOO *by Charlotte A. Eaton, Magdalene de Lancey & Juana Smith*—The Experiences of Three Women During the Campaign of 1815: Waterloo Days by Charlotte A. Eaton, A Week at Waterloo by Magdalene de Lancey & Juana's Story by Juana Smith.

JOURNAL OF AN OFFICER IN THE KING'S GERMAN LEGION *by John Frederick Hering*—Recollections of Campaigning During the Napoleonic Wars.

JOURNAL OF AN ARMY SURGEON IN THE PENINSULAR WAR *by Charles Boutflower*—The Recollections of a British Army Medical Man on Campaign During the Napoleonic Wars.

ON CAMPAIGN WITH MOORE AND WELLINGTON *by Anthony Hamilton*—The Experiences of a Soldier of the 43rd Regiment During the Peninsular War.

THE ROAD TO AUSTERLITZ *by R. G. Burton*—Napoleon's Campaign of 1805.

SOLDIERS OF NAPOLEON *by A. J. Doisy De Villargennes & Arthur Chuquet*—The Experiences of the Men of the French First Empire: Under the Eagles by A. J. Doisy De Villargennes & Voices of 1812 by Arthur Chuquet .

INVASION OF FRANCE, 1814 *by F. W. O. Maycock*—The Final Battles of the Napoleonic First Empire.

LEIPZIG—A CONFLICT OF TITANS *by Frederic Shoberl*—A Personal Experience of the 'Battle of the Nations' During the Napoleonic Wars, October 14th-19th, 1813.

SLASHERS *by Charles Cadell*—The Campaigns of the 28th Regiment of Foot During the Napoleonic Wars by a Serving Officer.

BATTLE IMPERIAL *by Charles William Vane*—The Campaigns in Germany & France for the Defeat of Napoleon 1813-1814.

SWIFT & BOLD *by Gibbes Rigaud*—The 60th Rifles During the Peninsula War.

www.ingramcontent.com/pod-product-compliance
Lightning Source LLC
Chambersburg PA
CBHW021100090426
42738CB00006B/436